50 Delicious Cookie Recipes for Home

By: Kelly Johnson

Table of Contents

- Chocolate Chip Cookies
- Classic Sugar Cookies
- Oatmeal Raisin Cookies
- Snickerdoodles
- Peanut Butter Cookies
- Double Chocolate Cookies
- White Chocolate Macadamia Nut Cookies
- Gingerbread Cookies
- Almond Joy Cookies
- Lemon Crinkle Cookies
- Red Velvet Cookies
- Mint Chocolate Chip Cookies
- Coconut Macaroons
- Pecan Sandies
- M&M Cookies
- Toffee Cookies
- Soft-Batch Chocolate Chip Cookies
- Cowboy Cookies
- Pumpkin Spice Cookies
- Molasses Cookies
- Nutella-Stuffed Cookies
- Caramel Apple Cookies
- Raspberry Jam Thumbprint Cookies
- Espresso Cookies
- Chocolate-Dipped Coconut Cookies
- S'mores Cookies
- Pumpkin Oatmeal Cookies
- Chai Spice Cookies
- Cranberry White Chocolate Cookies
- Maple Pecan Cookies
- Peanut Butter Blossoms
- Butterfinger Cookies
- Cheesecake Cookies
- Brookie Cookies (Brownie-Cookie Hybrid)
- Sea Salt Caramel Cookies
- Pretzel M&M Cookies

- Brown Butter Chocolate Chip Cookies
- Matcha Green Tea Cookies
- Puffed Rice Cookies
- Cherry Almond Cookies
- Apricot Almond Cookies
- Hazelnut Chocolate Cookies
- Espresso Chocolate Chip Cookies
- S'mores Sandwich Cookies
- Almond Butter Cookies
- Zucchini Cookies
- Vegan Chocolate Chip Cookies
- Gluten-Free Peanut Butter Cookies
- Strawberry Shortcake Cookies
- Chocolate Lava Cookies

Chocolate Chip Cookies

Ingredients:

- **Dry Ingredients:**
    - 2 1/4 cups all-purpose flour
    - 1/2 teaspoon baking soda
    - 1/2 teaspoon baking powder
    - 1/2 teaspoon salt
- **Wet Ingredients:**
    - 1 cup (2 sticks) unsalted butter, room temperature
    - 1/2 cup granulated sugar
    - 1 cup packed brown sugar
    - 1 teaspoon vanilla extract
    - 2 large eggs
- **Add-ins:**
    - 2 cups semisweet chocolate chips

Instructions:

1. **Preheat Oven:**
    - Preheat your oven to 350°F (175°C). Line baking sheets with parchment paper or silicone baking mats.
2. **Mix Dry Ingredients:**
    - In a medium bowl, whisk together flour, baking soda, baking powder, and salt. Set aside.
3. **Cream Butter and Sugars:**
    - In a large bowl, use an electric mixer to cream together the butter, granulated sugar, and brown sugar until light and fluffy, about 3 minutes.
4. **Add Eggs and Vanilla:**
    - Beat in the eggs one at a time, making sure each is fully incorporated before adding the next. Mix in the vanilla extract.
5. **Combine Wet and Dry Ingredients:**
    - Gradually add the dry ingredients to the wet ingredients, mixing just until combined. Do not overmix.
6. **Add Chocolate Chips:**
    - Stir in the chocolate chips until evenly distributed.
7. **Scoop Dough:**
    - Using a cookie scoop or tablespoon, drop rounded balls of dough onto the prepared baking sheets, spacing them about 2 inches apart.
8. **Bake:**
    - Bake in the preheated oven for 10-12 minutes, or until the edges are golden brown but the centers are still soft. Be careful not to overbake.
9. **Cool:**

- Allow the cookies to cool on the baking sheets for 5 minutes before transferring them to a wire rack to cool completely.

Tips:

- **Butter Temperature:** Ensure the butter is at room temperature for proper creaming.
- **Measuring Flour:** For best results, spoon the flour into the measuring cup and level it off, rather than scooping directly from the bag, to avoid overpacking.
- **Cookie Size:** For uniform cookies, use a cookie scoop or a tablespoon to portion out the dough.

Enjoy your freshly baked Chocolate Chip Cookies! These classic treats are always a hit.

Classic Sugar Cookies

Ingredients:

- **Dry Ingredients:**
    - 2 3/4 cups all-purpose flour
    - 1 1/2 teaspoons baking powder
    - 1/4 teaspoon salt
- **Wet Ingredients:**
    - 1 cup (2 sticks) unsalted butter, room temperature
    - 1 1/2 cups granulated sugar
    - 1 large egg
    - 1 teaspoon vanilla extract
- **For Rolling:**
    - Additional granulated sugar (for rolling the cookies)

Instructions:

1. **Preheat Oven:**
    - Preheat your oven to 375°F (190°C). Line baking sheets with parchment paper or silicone baking mats.
2. **Mix Dry Ingredients:**
    - In a medium bowl, whisk together the flour, baking powder, and salt. Set aside.
3. **Cream Butter and Sugar:**
    - In a large bowl, use an electric mixer to cream together the butter and granulated sugar until light and fluffy, about 3 minutes.
4. **Add Egg and Vanilla:**
    - Beat in the egg until well combined. Mix in the vanilla extract.
5. **Combine Wet and Dry Ingredients:**
    - Gradually add the dry ingredients to the wet ingredients, mixing just until combined. Do not overmix.
6. **Form Cookies:**
    - Roll rounded tablespoons of dough into balls and then roll them in granulated sugar. Place them on the prepared baking sheets, spacing them about 2 inches apart. Gently flatten each ball with the bottom of a glass or your hand.
7. **Bake:**
    - Bake in the preheated oven for 8-10 minutes, or until the edges are lightly golden. The centers may look a little soft but will set as they cool.
8. **Cool:**
    - Allow the cookies to cool on the baking sheets for about 5 minutes before transferring them to a wire rack to cool completely.

Tips:

- **Butter Temperature:** Ensure the butter is at room temperature for the best texture.
- **Cookie Size:** For consistent cookies, use a cookie scoop or measure the dough balls with a tablespoon.
- **Rolling in Sugar:** Rolling the dough balls in sugar before baking adds a nice texture and sweetness to the cookies.

Enjoy your Classic Sugar Cookies! They're perfect for decorating, gifting, or simply enjoying with a glass of milk.

Oatmeal Raisin Cookies

Ingredients:

- **Dry Ingredients:**
    - 1 1/2 cups all-purpose flour
    - 1 teaspoon baking soda
    - 1/2 teaspoon baking powder
    - 1/2 teaspoon salt
    - 1 teaspoon ground cinnamon
    - 1/4 teaspoon ground nutmeg (optional)
- **Wet Ingredients:**
    - 1 cup (2 sticks) unsalted butter, room temperature
    - 1 cup granulated sugar
    - 1 cup packed brown sugar
    - 2 large eggs
    - 1 teaspoon vanilla extract
- **Add-ins:**
    - 3 cups old-fashioned rolled oats
    - 1 cup raisins (or currants, if preferred)
    - 1/2 cup chopped nuts (optional, such as walnuts or pecans)

Instructions:

1. **Preheat Oven:**
    - Preheat your oven to 350°F (175°C). Line baking sheets with parchment paper or silicone baking mats.
2. **Mix Dry Ingredients:**
    - In a medium bowl, whisk together flour, baking soda, baking powder, salt, cinnamon, and nutmeg. Set aside.
3. **Cream Butter and Sugars:**
    - In a large bowl, use an electric mixer to cream together the butter, granulated sugar, and brown sugar until light and fluffy, about 3 minutes.
4. **Add Eggs and Vanilla:**
    - Beat in the eggs one at a time, ensuring each is fully incorporated before adding the next. Mix in the vanilla extract.
5. **Combine Wet and Dry Ingredients:**
    - Gradually add the dry ingredients to the wet ingredients, mixing just until combined.
6. **Add Oats, Raisins, and Nuts:**
    - Stir in the oats, raisins, and nuts (if using) until evenly distributed.
7. **Form Cookies:**

- Using a cookie scoop or tablespoon, drop rounded balls of dough onto the prepared baking sheets, spacing them about 2 inches apart. Flatten the dough balls slightly with the back of a spoon.

8. **Bake:**
   - Bake in the preheated oven for 10-12 minutes, or until the edges are golden brown and the centers are set. The cookies may still look slightly soft in the center but will firm up as they cool.
9. **Cool:**
   - Allow the cookies to cool on the baking sheets for about 5 minutes before transferring them to a wire rack to cool completely.

Tips:

- **Butter Temperature:** Ensure the butter is at room temperature for the best mixing and texture.
- **Oats:** Use old-fashioned rolled oats for the best texture. Quick oats can be used, but the texture will be slightly different.
- **Raisins:** For plumper raisins, you can soak them in warm water for 10 minutes before using.

Enjoy your homemade Oatmeal Raisin Cookies! They're great for a snack, dessert, or a lunchbox treat.

Snickerdoodles

Ingredients:

- **Dry Ingredients:**
    - 2 3/4 cups all-purpose flour
    - 1/2 teaspoon baking soda
    - 1/2 teaspoon cream of tartar
    - 1/4 teaspoon salt
- **Wet Ingredients:**
    - 1 cup (2 sticks) unsalted butter, room temperature
    - 1 1/2 cups granulated sugar
    - 2 large eggs
    - 1 teaspoon vanilla extract
- **Cinnamon-Sugar Coating:**
    - 3 tablespoons granulated sugar
    - 1 tablespoon ground cinnamon

Instructions:

1. **Preheat Oven:**
    - Preheat your oven to 350°F (175°C). Line baking sheets with parchment paper or silicone baking mats.
2. **Mix Dry Ingredients:**
    - In a medium bowl, whisk together flour, baking soda, cream of tartar, and salt. Set aside.
3. **Cream Butter and Sugar:**
    - In a large bowl, use an electric mixer to cream together the butter and granulated sugar until light and fluffy, about 3 minutes.
4. **Add Eggs and Vanilla:**
    - Beat in the eggs one at a time, making sure each is fully incorporated before adding the next. Mix in the vanilla extract.
5. **Combine Wet and Dry Ingredients:**
    - Gradually add the dry ingredients to the wet ingredients, mixing just until combined.
6. **Prepare Cinnamon-Sugar Coating:**
    - In a small bowl, mix together 3 tablespoons of granulated sugar and 1 tablespoon of ground cinnamon.
7. **Form Cookies:**
    - Roll rounded tablespoons of dough into balls and then roll them in the cinnamon-sugar mixture. Place the coated dough balls on the prepared baking sheets, spacing them about 2 inches apart.
8. **Bake:**

- Bake in the preheated oven for 10-12 minutes, or until the edges are lightly golden. The centers should look soft but set.
9. **Cool:**
    - Allow the cookies to cool on the baking sheets for about 5 minutes before transferring them to a wire rack to cool completely.

Tips:

- **Butter Temperature:** Make sure the butter is at room temperature for the best texture and consistency in your cookies.
- **Cream of Tartar:** This ingredient gives Snickerdoodles their signature tangy flavor and chewy texture. If you don't have cream of tartar, you can substitute with 1 teaspoon of baking powder, but the flavor will be slightly different.
- **Rolling:** Rolling the dough balls in cinnamon-sugar before baking ensures a lovely coating and adds to the cookies' distinctive flavor.

Enjoy your homemade Snickerdoodles! They're perfect for a sweet treat with a cup of tea or coffee.

Peanut Butter Cookies

Ingredients:

- **Dry Ingredients:**
    - 1 1/2 cups all-purpose flour
    - 1/2 teaspoon baking soda
    - 1/2 teaspoon baking powder
    - 1/4 teaspoon salt
- **Wet Ingredients:**
    - 1 cup (2 sticks) unsalted butter, room temperature
    - 1 cup creamy or chunky peanut butter (make sure it's well-stirred)
    - 1 cup granulated sugar
    - 1 cup packed brown sugar
    - 1 large egg
    - 1 teaspoon vanilla extract

Instructions:

1. **Preheat Oven:**
    - Preheat your oven to 350°F (175°C). Line baking sheets with parchment paper or silicone baking mats.
2. **Mix Dry Ingredients:**
    - In a medium bowl, whisk together flour, baking soda, baking powder, and salt. Set aside.
3. **Cream Butter, Peanut Butter, and Sugars:**
    - In a large bowl, use an electric mixer to cream together the butter, peanut butter, granulated sugar, and brown sugar until light and fluffy, about 3 minutes.
4. **Add Egg and Vanilla:**
    - Beat in the egg until fully combined. Mix in the vanilla extract.
5. **Combine Wet and Dry Ingredients:**
    - Gradually add the dry ingredients to the wet ingredients, mixing just until combined.
6. **Form Cookies:**
    - Using a cookie scoop or tablespoon, drop rounded balls of dough onto the prepared baking sheets, spacing them about 2 inches apart. Use a fork to flatten each dough ball and create a crisscross pattern on top.
7. **Bake:**
    - Bake in the preheated oven for 10-12 minutes, or until the edges are lightly golden. The centers should look slightly soft but will firm up as they cool.
8. **Cool:**
    - Allow the cookies to cool on the baking sheets for about 5 minutes before transferring them to a wire rack to cool completely.

Tips:

- **Peanut Butter:** You can use either creamy or chunky peanut butter depending on your texture preference. Make sure it's well-stirred if using natural peanut butter.
- **Fork Marks:** Pressing down with a fork helps to flatten the cookies and creates the classic crisscross pattern. For a more uniform shape, you can also use a cookie scoop.
- **Storage:** Store the cookies in an airtight container at room temperature for up to a week or freeze them for longer storage.

Enjoy your homemade Peanut Butter Cookies! They're perfect for a snack or a sweet treat with a glass of milk.

Double Chocolate Cookies

Ingredients:

- **Dry Ingredients:**
    - 1 3/4 cups all-purpose flour
    - 1/2 cup unsweetened cocoa powder
    - 1 teaspoon baking soda
    - 1/2 teaspoon baking powder
    - 1/4 teaspoon salt
- **Wet Ingredients:**
    - 1 cup (2 sticks) unsalted butter, room temperature
    - 1 cup granulated sugar
    - 1 cup packed brown sugar
    - 2 large eggs
    - 2 teaspoons vanilla extract
- **Add-ins:**
    - 1 cup semisweet chocolate chips (or chunks)
    - 1/2 cup white chocolate chips (optional, for extra chocolate flavor and texture)

Instructions:

1. **Preheat Oven:**
    - Preheat your oven to 350°F (175°C). Line baking sheets with parchment paper or silicone baking mats.
2. **Mix Dry Ingredients:**
    - In a medium bowl, whisk together flour, cocoa powder, baking soda, baking powder, and salt. Set aside.
3. **Cream Butter and Sugars:**
    - In a large bowl, use an electric mixer to cream together the butter, granulated sugar, and brown sugar until light and fluffy, about 3 minutes.
4. **Add Eggs and Vanilla:**
    - Beat in the eggs one at a time, making sure each is fully incorporated before adding the next. Mix in the vanilla extract.
5. **Combine Wet and Dry Ingredients:**
    - Gradually add the dry ingredients to the wet ingredients, mixing just until combined.
6. **Add Chocolate Chips:**
    - Stir in the semisweet chocolate chips and white chocolate chips (if using) until evenly distributed.
7. **Form Cookies:**
    - Using a cookie scoop or tablespoon, drop rounded balls of dough onto the prepared baking sheets, spacing them about 2 inches apart.
8. **Bake:**

- Bake in the preheated oven for 10-12 minutes, or until the edges are set and the centers are still soft. The cookies will continue to firm up as they cool.

9. **Cool:**
   - Allow the cookies to cool on the baking sheets for about 5 minutes before transferring them to a wire rack to cool completely.

Tips:

- **Butter Temperature:** Ensure the butter is at room temperature for the best mixing and texture.
- **Cocoa Powder:** Use high-quality unsweetened cocoa powder for a richer chocolate flavor.
- **Chocolate Chips:** Feel free to use your favorite type of chocolate chips or chunks, and you can mix and match with milk chocolate, dark chocolate, or even flavored chips.

Enjoy your homemade Double Chocolate Cookies! They're perfect for satisfying a chocolate craving and make a great treat for sharing or gifting.

White Chocolate Macadamia Nut Cookies

Ingredients:

- **Dry Ingredients:**
    - 2 1/4 cups all-purpose flour
    - 1/2 teaspoon baking soda
    - 1/2 teaspoon baking powder
    - 1/4 teaspoon salt
- **Wet Ingredients:**
    - 1 cup (2 sticks) unsalted butter, room temperature
    - 1 cup granulated sugar
    - 1 cup packed brown sugar
    - 2 large eggs
    - 1 teaspoon vanilla extract
- **Add-ins:**
    - 1 cup white chocolate chips
    - 1 cup macadamia nuts, chopped (lightly toasted, if desired)

Instructions:

1. **Preheat Oven:**
    - Preheat your oven to 350°F (175°C). Line baking sheets with parchment paper or silicone baking mats.
2. **Mix Dry Ingredients:**
    - In a medium bowl, whisk together the flour, baking soda, baking powder, and salt. Set aside.
3. **Cream Butter and Sugars:**
    - In a large bowl, use an electric mixer to cream together the butter, granulated sugar, and brown sugar until light and fluffy, about 3 minutes.
4. **Add Eggs and Vanilla:**
    - Beat in the eggs one at a time, making sure each is fully incorporated before adding the next. Mix in the vanilla extract.
5. **Combine Wet and Dry Ingredients:**
    - Gradually add the dry ingredients to the wet ingredients, mixing just until combined.
6. **Add White Chocolate and Nuts:**
    - Stir in the white chocolate chips and chopped macadamia nuts until evenly distributed.
7. **Form Cookies:**
    - Using a cookie scoop or tablespoon, drop rounded balls of dough onto the prepared baking sheets, spacing them about 2 inches apart.
8. **Bake:**

- Bake in the preheated oven for 10-12 minutes, or until the edges are lightly golden. The centers should look slightly soft but will firm up as they cool.
9. **Cool:**
   - Allow the cookies to cool on the baking sheets for about 5 minutes before transferring them to a wire rack to cool completely.

Tips:

- **Butter Temperature:** Make sure the butter is at room temperature for the best texture and mixing.
- **Macadamia Nuts:** Toasting the macadamia nuts lightly can enhance their flavor, but it's optional.
- **White Chocolate:** If using large white chocolate chunks, you may need to chop them into smaller pieces to distribute them more evenly.

Enjoy your homemade White Chocolate Macadamia Nut Cookies! They're perfect for a sweet treat, gifting, or sharing with friends and family.

Gingerbread Cookies

Ingredients:

- **Dry Ingredients:**
    - 3 1/4 cups all-purpose flour
    - 1 teaspoon baking soda
    - 1 tablespoon ground ginger
    - 1 tablespoon ground cinnamon
    - 1/2 teaspoon ground cloves
    - 1/4 teaspoon ground nutmeg
    - 1/4 teaspoon salt
- **Wet Ingredients:**
    - 1/2 cup (1 stick) unsalted butter, room temperature
    - 1/2 cup granulated sugar
    - 1/2 cup packed brown sugar
    - 1 large egg
    - 1/2 cup unsulfured molasses
    - 1 teaspoon vanilla extract

Optional for Decoration:

- **Royal Icing:**
    - 1 egg white (or 2 tablespoons egg white powder mixed with 2 tablespoons water)
    - 2 cups powdered sugar
    - 1/2 teaspoon lemon juice

Instructions:

1. **Preheat Oven:**
    - Preheat your oven to 350°F (175°C). Line baking sheets with parchment paper or silicone baking mats.
2. **Mix Dry Ingredients:**
    - In a medium bowl, whisk together flour, baking soda, ginger, cinnamon, cloves, nutmeg, and salt. Set aside.
3. **Cream Butter and Sugars:**
    - In a large bowl, use an electric mixer to cream together the butter, granulated sugar, and brown sugar until light and fluffy, about 3 minutes.
4. **Add Egg, Molasses, and Vanilla:**
    - Beat in the egg until well combined. Mix in the molasses and vanilla extract.
5. **Combine Wet and Dry Ingredients:**
    - Gradually add the dry ingredients to the wet ingredients, mixing just until combined. The dough will be thick.
6. **Chill Dough:**

- Divide the dough into two portions, wrap them in plastic wrap, and chill in the refrigerator for at least 1 hour. This makes the dough easier to roll out.

7. **Roll Out and Cut Cookies:**
   - On a lightly floured surface, roll out one portion of dough to about 1/8-inch thickness. Use cookie cutters to cut out desired shapes and place them on the prepared baking sheets.

8. **Bake:**
   - Bake in the preheated oven for 8-10 minutes, or until the edges are firm and the centers are set. The cookies will firm up as they cool.

9. **Cool:**
   - Allow the cookies to cool on the baking sheets for about 5 minutes before transferring them to a wire rack to cool completely.

10. **Decorate (Optional):**
    - If using royal icing, beat the egg white until frothy. Gradually add powdered sugar and lemon juice, and beat until stiff peaks form. Decorate cooled cookies with the icing and let dry completely.

Tips:

- **Chilling Dough:** Chilling the dough helps prevent the cookies from spreading and maintains their shape.
- **Rolling Dough:** Use a lightly floured rolling pin and surface to prevent sticking.
- **Decorating:** If decorating, ensure the cookies are completely cooled to avoid smudging the icing.

Enjoy your homemade Gingerbread Cookies! They're perfect for holiday decorating, gifting, or simply enjoying with a cup of tea or milk.

Almond Joy Cookies

Ingredients:

- **Dry Ingredients:**
    - 1 3/4 cups all-purpose flour
    - 1/2 teaspoon baking soda
    - 1/4 teaspoon salt
- **Wet Ingredients:**
    - 1/2 cup (1 stick) unsalted butter, room temperature
    - 1/2 cup granulated sugar
    - 1/2 cup packed brown sugar
    - 1 large egg
    - 1 teaspoon vanilla extract
- **Add-ins:**
    - 1 cup shredded sweetened coconut
    - 1/2 cup semisweet chocolate chips (or chunks)
    - 1/2 cup whole almonds (lightly toasted, if desired)

Instructions:

1. **Preheat Oven:**
    - Preheat your oven to 350°F (175°C). Line baking sheets with parchment paper or silicone baking mats.
2. **Mix Dry Ingredients:**
    - In a medium bowl, whisk together flour, baking soda, and salt. Set aside.
3. **Cream Butter and Sugars:**
    - In a large bowl, use an electric mixer to cream together the butter, granulated sugar, and brown sugar until light and fluffy, about 3 minutes.
4. **Add Egg and Vanilla:**
    - Beat in the egg until well combined. Mix in the vanilla extract.
5. **Combine Wet and Dry Ingredients:**
    - Gradually add the dry ingredients to the wet ingredients, mixing just until combined.
6. **Add Coconut, Chocolate Chips, and Almonds:**
    - Fold in the shredded coconut, chocolate chips, and whole almonds until evenly distributed.
7. **Form Cookies:**
    - Using a cookie scoop or tablespoon, drop rounded balls of dough onto the prepared baking sheets, spacing them about 2 inches apart. Press an extra almond into the top of each cookie for decoration, if desired.
8. **Bake:**
    - Bake in the preheated oven for 10-12 minutes, or until the edges are lightly golden. The centers should be set but slightly soft.

9. **Cool:**
    - Allow the cookies to cool on the baking sheets for about 5 minutes before transferring them to a wire rack to cool completely.

Tips:

- **Butter Temperature:** Ensure the butter is at room temperature for the best mixing and texture in your cookies.
- **Coconut:** Use sweetened shredded coconut for the best flavor and texture. If you prefer a less sweet cookie, you can use unsweetened coconut.
- **Almonds:** Toasting the almonds lightly can enhance their flavor, but it's optional.

Enjoy your homemade Almond Joy Cookies! They're a great way to indulge in the flavors of the classic candy bar in cookie form.

Lemon Crinkle Cookies

Ingredients:

- **Dry Ingredients:**
    - 2 cups all-purpose flour
    - 1/2 teaspoon baking powder
    - 1/2 teaspoon baking soda
    - 1/4 teaspoon salt
- **Wet Ingredients:**
    - 1/2 cup (1 stick) unsalted butter, room temperature
    - 1 cup granulated sugar
    - 1 large egg
    - 2 tablespoons fresh lemon juice (about 1 lemon)
    - 1 tablespoon lemon zest (from about 1 lemon)
    - 1 teaspoon vanilla extract
- **Coating:**
    - 1/2 cup granulated sugar
    - 1/2 cup powdered sugar

Instructions:

1. **Preheat Oven:**
    - Preheat your oven to 350°F (175°C). Line baking sheets with parchment paper or silicone baking mats.
2. **Mix Dry Ingredients:**
    - In a medium bowl, whisk together flour, baking powder, baking soda, and salt. Set aside.
3. **Cream Butter and Sugar:**
    - In a large bowl, use an electric mixer to cream together the butter and granulated sugar until light and fluffy, about 3 minutes.
4. **Add Egg, Lemon Juice, Lemon Zest, and Vanilla:**
    - Beat in the egg until fully combined. Mix in the lemon juice, lemon zest, and vanilla extract.
5. **Combine Wet and Dry Ingredients:**
    - Gradually add the dry ingredients to the wet ingredients, mixing just until combined.
6. **Prepare Coating:**
    - In a small bowl, combine the granulated sugar and powdered sugar for coating.
7. **Form Cookies:**
    - Using a cookie scoop or tablespoon, scoop rounded balls of dough and roll them in the sugar mixture to coat. Place the coated dough balls on the prepared baking sheets, spacing them about 2 inches apart.
8. **Bake:**

- Bake in the preheated oven for 10-12 minutes, or until the edges are lightly golden and the centers are set. The cookies will continue to firm up as they cool.
9. **Cool:**
    - Allow the cookies to cool on the baking sheets for about 5 minutes before transferring them to a wire rack to cool completely.

Tips:

- **Butter Temperature:** Make sure the butter is at room temperature to achieve the best texture and mixing.
- **Lemon Zest:** Use a fine grater to zest the lemon to avoid large pieces of zest in the dough.
- **Coating:** Rolling the cookies in the sugar mixture before baking helps create the crinkled appearance.

Enjoy your homemade Lemon Crinkle Cookies! They're perfect for adding a fresh, citrusy twist to your cookie collection.

Red Velvet Cookies

Ingredients:

- **Dry Ingredients:**
    - 2 1/4 cups all-purpose flour
    - 1/2 teaspoon baking soda
    - 1/4 teaspoon salt
    - 2 tablespoons unsweetened cocoa powder
- **Wet Ingredients:**
    - 1 cup (2 sticks) unsalted butter, room temperature
    - 1 cup granulated sugar
    - 1/2 cup packed brown sugar
    - 1 large egg
    - 2 tablespoons red food coloring (gel or liquid)
    - 1 teaspoon vanilla extract
    - 1 teaspoon white vinegar (optional, for a slight tang)
- **Optional:**
    - 1 cup white chocolate chips or semisweet chocolate chips for added sweetness and texture

Instructions:

1. Preheat Oven:
    - Preheat your oven to 350°F (175°C). Line baking sheets with parchment paper or silicone baking mats.
2. Mix Dry Ingredients:
    - In a medium bowl, whisk together flour, baking soda, salt, and cocoa powder. Set aside.
3. Cream Butter and Sugars:
    - In a large bowl, use an electric mixer to cream together the butter, granulated sugar, and brown sugar until light and fluffy, about 3 minutes.
4. Add Egg, Food Coloring, Vanilla, and Vinegar:
    - Beat in the egg until well combined. Mix in the red food coloring, vanilla extract, and vinegar (if using). The mixture should be a vibrant red color.
5. Combine Wet and Dry Ingredients:
    - Gradually add the dry ingredients to the wet ingredients, mixing just until combined. If using, fold in the white chocolate chips or semisweet chocolate chips.
6. Form Cookies:
    - Using a cookie scoop or tablespoon, drop rounded balls of dough onto the prepared baking sheets, spacing them about 2 inches apart.
7. Bake:

- Bake in the preheated oven for 10-12 minutes, or until the edges are set and the centers are just slightly soft. The cookies will firm up as they cool.
8. Cool:
    - Allow the cookies to cool on the baking sheets for about 5 minutes before transferring them to a wire rack to cool completely.

Tips:

- Butter Temperature: Ensure the butter is at room temperature for optimal texture and consistency in your cookies.
- Food Coloring: Use gel food coloring for a more intense red color, if desired. Liquid food coloring works as well but may require more to achieve the same intensity.
- Vinegar: The vinegar is optional but can help mimic the slight tanginess of red velvet cake.

Enjoy your homemade Red Velvet Cookies! They're a delightful treat with a rich, distinctive flavor and striking color.

Mint Chocolate Chip Cookies

Ingredients:

- **Dry Ingredients:**
    - 2 1/4 cups all-purpose flour
    - 1/2 teaspoon baking soda
    - 1/4 teaspoon salt
- **Wet Ingredients:**
    - 1 cup (2 sticks) unsalted butter, room temperature
    - 1 cup granulated sugar
    - 1 cup packed brown sugar
    - 2 large eggs
    - 1 teaspoon vanilla extract
    - 1 teaspoon peppermint extract (adjust to taste)
- **Add-ins:**
    - 1 cup semisweet chocolate chips
    - 1/2 cup crushed peppermint candies or candy canes (optional, for extra crunch)

Instructions:

1. Preheat Oven:
    - Preheat your oven to 350°F (175°C). Line baking sheets with parchment paper or silicone baking mats.
2. Mix Dry Ingredients:
    - In a medium bowl, whisk together flour, baking soda, and salt. Set aside.
3. Cream Butter and Sugars:
    - In a large bowl, use an electric mixer to cream together the butter, granulated sugar, and brown sugar until light and fluffy, about 3 minutes.
4. Add Eggs, Vanilla, and Peppermint Extract:
    - Beat in the eggs one at a time, mixing well after each addition. Then mix in the vanilla extract and peppermint extract.
5. Combine Wet and Dry Ingredients:
    - Gradually add the dry ingredients to the wet ingredients, mixing just until combined.
6. Add Chocolate Chips and Peppermint Candies:
    - Fold in the chocolate chips and crushed peppermint candies if using.
7. Form Cookies:
    - Using a cookie scoop or tablespoon, drop rounded balls of dough onto the prepared baking sheets, spacing them about 2 inches apart.
8. Bake:
    - Bake in the preheated oven for 10-12 minutes, or until the edges are lightly golden and the centers are just set.
9. Cool:

- Allow the cookies to cool on the baking sheets for about 5 minutes before transferring them to a wire rack to cool completely.

Tips:

- Peppermint Extract: Start with 1 teaspoon and adjust to your taste. Peppermint extract can be quite strong, so add in small increments if you prefer a milder mint flavor.
- Peppermint Candies: Crush peppermint candies using a rolling pin or food processor for a more even texture, or leave them in larger chunks for added crunch.
- Butter Temperature: Ensure the butter is at room temperature to get the best texture and consistency in your cookies.

Enjoy these homemade Mint Chocolate Chip Cookies! They're perfect for a fresh and festive twist on a classic chocolate chip cookie.

Coconut Macaroons

Ingredients:

- **For the Macaroons:**
    - 14 ounces (about 4 cups) sweetened shredded coconut
    - 1 cup sweetened condensed milk (one 14-ounce can)
    - 1 teaspoon vanilla extract
    - 1/4 teaspoon almond extract (optional, for added flavor)
    - 2 large egg whites
    - 1/4 teaspoon salt
- **For Dipping (Optional):**
    - 1 cup semisweet or dark chocolate chips
    - 1 teaspoon vegetable oil (for melting the chocolate)

Instructions:

1. **Preheat Oven:**
    - Preheat your oven to 325°F (165°C). Line a baking sheet with parchment paper or a silicone baking mat.
2. **Mix Coconut Ingredients:**
    - In a large bowl, combine the shredded coconut, sweetened condensed milk, vanilla extract, and almond extract (if using). Stir until well mixed.
3. **Beat Egg Whites:**
    - In a separate clean bowl, use an electric mixer to beat the egg whites and salt until stiff peaks form.
4. **Fold in Egg Whites:**
    - Gently fold the beaten egg whites into the coconut mixture. Be careful not to deflate the egg whites too much; fold until just combined.
5. **Form Macaroons:**
    - Using a cookie scoop or tablespoon, drop rounded mounds of the mixture onto the prepared baking sheet, spacing them about 1 inch apart.
6. **Bake:**
    - Bake in the preheated oven for 15-20 minutes, or until the edges are golden brown. The centers will remain soft and chewy.
7. **Cool:**
    - Allow the macaroons to cool on the baking sheet for a few minutes before transferring them to a wire rack to cool completely.
8. **Optional Chocolate Dip:**
    - If you'd like to dip your macaroons in chocolate, melt the chocolate chips with the vegetable oil in a microwave-safe bowl in 30-second intervals, stirring in between until smooth.
    - Dip the cooled macaroons halfway into the melted chocolate and place them on parchment paper to set. Allow the chocolate to harden before serving.

Tips:

- **Shredded Coconut:** Use sweetened shredded coconut for the best flavor. If you prefer a less sweet macaroon, you can use unsweetened shredded coconut and adjust the sweetness with more sweetened condensed milk.
- **Egg Whites:** Make sure your mixing bowl and beaters are completely clean and dry to achieve stiff peaks with the egg whites.
- **Chocolate Dipping:** If the chocolate is too thick for dipping, you can add a little more vegetable oil to thin it out.

Enjoy your homemade Coconut Macaroons! They're perfect for a sweet treat or for sharing with family and friends.

Pecan Sandies

Ingredients:

- **Dry Ingredients:**
    - 2 1/4 cups all-purpose flour
    - 1/2 teaspoon baking soda
    - 1/4 teaspoon salt
- **Wet Ingredients:**
    - 1 cup (2 sticks) unsalted butter, room temperature
    - 1 cup granulated sugar
    - 1/2 cup packed brown sugar
    - 1 large egg
    - 1 teaspoon vanilla extract
- **Add-ins:**
    - 1 cup chopped pecans (toasted if desired)

Instructions:

1. **Preheat Oven:**
    - Preheat your oven to 350°F (175°C). Line baking sheets with parchment paper or silicone baking mats.
2. **Toast Pecans (Optional):**
    - If you prefer toasted pecans, spread the chopped pecans on a baking sheet and toast them in the preheated oven for 5-7 minutes, or until fragrant. Allow to cool before using.
3. **Mix Dry Ingredients:**
    - In a medium bowl, whisk together flour, baking soda, and salt. Set aside.
4. **Cream Butter and Sugars:**
    - In a large bowl, use an electric mixer to cream together the butter, granulated sugar, and brown sugar until light and fluffy, about 3 minutes.
5. **Add Egg and Vanilla:**
    - Beat in the egg until well combined. Mix in the vanilla extract.
6. **Combine Wet and Dry Ingredients:**
    - Gradually add the dry ingredients to the wet ingredients, mixing just until combined.
7. **Fold in Pecans:**
    - Fold in the chopped pecans until evenly distributed throughout the dough.
8. **Form Cookies:**
    - Using a cookie scoop or tablespoon, drop rounded balls of dough onto the prepared baking sheets, spacing them about 2 inches apart. Flatten each ball slightly with the palm of your hand or the bottom of a glass.
9. **Bake:**

- - Bake in the preheated oven for 10-12 minutes, or until the edges are lightly golden. The centers should be set but soft.
10. **Cool:**
    - Allow the cookies to cool on the baking sheets for about 5 minutes before transferring them to a wire rack to cool completely.

Tips:

- **Butter Temperature:** Ensure the butter is at room temperature for the best texture and consistency in your cookies.
- **Pecans:** Toasting the pecans enhances their flavor but is optional. If you prefer a softer nutty taste, you can use them raw.
- **Flattening Cookies:** Flattening the dough balls slightly before baking helps the cookies spread evenly and achieve a nice, uniform shape.

Enjoy your homemade Pecan Sandies! They're a delightful and nutty treat that pairs perfectly with a cup of tea or coffee.

M&M Cookies

Ingredients:

- **Dry Ingredients:**
    - 2 1/4 cups all-purpose flour
    - 1/2 teaspoon baking soda
    - 1/2 teaspoon baking powder
    - 1/4 teaspoon salt
- **Wet Ingredients:**
    - 1 cup (2 sticks) unsalted butter, room temperature
    - 1 cup granulated sugar
    - 1 cup packed brown sugar
    - 2 large eggs
    - 1 teaspoon vanilla extract
- **Add-ins:**
    - 1 1/2 cups M&Ms (plain or peanut, depending on your preference)

Instructions:

1. **Preheat Oven:**
    - Preheat your oven to 350°F (175°C). Line baking sheets with parchment paper or silicone baking mats.
2. **Mix Dry Ingredients:**
    - In a medium bowl, whisk together flour, baking soda, baking powder, and salt. Set aside.
3. **Cream Butter and Sugars:**
    - In a large bowl, use an electric mixer to cream together the butter, granulated sugar, and brown sugar until light and fluffy, about 3 minutes.
4. **Add Eggs and Vanilla:**
    - Beat in the eggs one at a time until fully incorporated. Mix in the vanilla extract.
5. **Combine Wet and Dry Ingredients:**
    - Gradually add the dry ingredients to the wet ingredients, mixing just until combined.
6. **Fold in M&Ms:**
    - Gently fold in the M&Ms until evenly distributed throughout the dough.
7. **Form Cookies:**
    - Using a cookie scoop or tablespoon, drop rounded balls of dough onto the prepared baking sheets, spacing them about 2 inches apart. Press a few extra M&Ms into the tops of the cookies for a more colorful appearance, if desired.
8. **Bake:**
    - Bake in the preheated oven for 10-12 minutes, or until the edges are lightly golden and the centers are set. The cookies will continue to firm up as they cool.
9. **Cool:**

- Allow the cookies to cool on the baking sheets for about 5 minutes before transferring them to a wire rack to cool completely.

Tips:

- **Butter Temperature:** Make sure the butter is at room temperature for the best texture in your cookies.
- **M&Ms:** You can use any type of M&Ms you prefer, whether classic plain, peanut, or even mini M&Ms.
- **Extra M&Ms:** Pressing extra M&Ms into the tops of the cookies before baking helps them look more appealing and colorful.

Enjoy your homemade M&M Cookies! They're a cheerful and delicious treat that's sure to brighten up anyone's day.

Toffee Cookies

Ingredients:

- **Dry Ingredients:**
    - 2 1/4 cups all-purpose flour
    - 1/2 teaspoon baking soda
    - 1/2 teaspoon baking powder
    - 1/4 teaspoon salt
- **Wet Ingredients:**
    - 1 cup (2 sticks) unsalted butter, room temperature
    - 1 cup granulated sugar
    - 1/2 cup packed brown sugar
    - 2 large eggs
    - 1 teaspoon vanilla extract
- **Add-ins:**
    - 1 cup toffee bits or chopped toffee bars (such as Heath Bar)

Instructions:

1. **Preheat Oven:**
    - Preheat your oven to 350°F (175°C). Line baking sheets with parchment paper or silicone baking mats.
2. **Mix Dry Ingredients:**
    - In a medium bowl, whisk together flour, baking soda, baking powder, and salt. Set aside.
3. **Cream Butter and Sugars:**
    - In a large bowl, use an electric mixer to cream together the butter, granulated sugar, and brown sugar until light and fluffy, about 3 minutes.
4. **Add Eggs and Vanilla:**
    - Beat in the eggs one at a time until fully incorporated. Mix in the vanilla extract.
5. **Combine Wet and Dry Ingredients:**
    - Gradually add the dry ingredients to the wet ingredients, mixing just until combined.
6. **Fold in Toffee Bits:**
    - Gently fold in the toffee bits until evenly distributed throughout the dough.
7. **Form Cookies:**
    - Using a cookie scoop or tablespoon, drop rounded balls of dough onto the prepared baking sheets, spacing them about 2 inches apart.
8. **Bake:**
    - Bake in the preheated oven for 10-12 minutes, or until the edges are lightly golden and the centers are set. The cookies will continue to firm up as they cool.
9. **Cool:**

- Allow the cookies to cool on the baking sheets for about 5 minutes before transferring them to a wire rack to cool completely.

Tips:

- **Butter Temperature:** Ensure the butter is at room temperature for a smooth and creamy dough.
- **Toffee Bits:** Toffee bits can be found in most grocery stores, often in the baking aisle. If using chopped toffee bars, make sure they are chopped into small pieces to distribute evenly in the dough.
- **Cookie Size:** For uniform cookies, use a cookie scoop or spoon to ensure each cookie is the same size.

Enjoy your homemade Toffee Cookies! They're a sweet and buttery treat with a satisfying crunch from the toffee bits.

Soft-Batch Chocolate Chip Cookies

Ingredients:

- **Dry Ingredients:**
    - 2 1/4 cups all-purpose flour
    - 1/2 teaspoon baking soda
    - 1/4 teaspoon baking powder
    - 1/2 teaspoon salt
- **Wet Ingredients:**
    - 1 cup (2 sticks) unsalted butter, room temperature
    - 1 cup granulated sugar
    - 1 cup packed brown sugar
    - 2 large eggs
    - 2 teaspoons vanilla extract
- **Add-ins:**
    - 1 1/2 cups semisweet chocolate chips

Instructions:

1. **Preheat Oven:**
    - Preheat your oven to 350°F (175°C). Line baking sheets with parchment paper or silicone baking mats.
2. **Mix Dry Ingredients:**
    - In a medium bowl, whisk together flour, baking soda, baking powder, and salt. Set aside.
3. **Cream Butter and Sugars:**
    - In a large bowl, use an electric mixer to cream together the butter, granulated sugar, and brown sugar until light and fluffy, about 3 minutes.
4. **Add Eggs and Vanilla:**
    - Beat in the eggs one at a time until fully incorporated. Mix in the vanilla extract.
5. **Combine Wet and Dry Ingredients:**
    - Gradually add the dry ingredients to the wet ingredients, mixing just until combined. Avoid overmixing.
6. **Fold in Chocolate Chips:**
    - Gently fold in the chocolate chips until evenly distributed throughout the dough.
7. **Form Cookies:**
    - Using a cookie scoop or tablespoon, drop rounded balls of dough onto the prepared baking sheets, spacing them about 2 inches apart. The dough will spread slightly but not too much.
8. **Bake:**
    - Bake in the preheated oven for 10-12 minutes, or until the edges are lightly golden but the centers are still soft and slightly underbaked.
9. **Cool:**

- Allow the cookies to cool on the baking sheets for about 5 minutes before transferring them to a wire rack to cool completely. They will continue to set as they cool.

Tips:

- **Butter Temperature:** Ensure the butter is at room temperature for the best texture in your cookies.
- **Chocolate Chips:** You can use semisweet, milk, or dark chocolate chips based on your preference. For a twist, try adding chunks of your favorite chocolate bar.
- **Do Not Overbake:** For the softest cookies, remove them from the oven when the edges are golden but the centers are still soft. They will continue to cook slightly on the baking sheets.

Enjoy your homemade Soft-Batch Chocolate Chip Cookies! They're perfect for a comforting treat and are sure to satisfy your cookie cravings with their soft, chewy texture and rich chocolate flavor.

Cowboy Cookies

Ingredients:

- **Dry Ingredients:**
    - 1 1/2 cups all-purpose flour
    - 1 teaspoon baking powder
    - 1/2 teaspoon baking soda
    - 1/4 teaspoon salt
    - 1 cup old-fashioned rolled oats
- **Wet Ingredients:**
    - 1 cup (2 sticks) unsalted butter, room temperature
    - 1 cup granulated sugar
    - 1 cup packed brown sugar
    - 2 large eggs
    - 1 teaspoon vanilla extract
- **Add-ins:**
    - 1 cup semisweet chocolate chips
    - 1/2 cup chopped nuts (such as pecans or walnuts)
    - 1/2 cup sweetened shredded coconut
    - 1/2 cup raisins or dried cranberries (optional)

Instructions:

1. **Preheat Oven:**
    - Preheat your oven to 350°F (175°C). Line baking sheets with parchment paper or silicone baking mats.
2. **Mix Dry Ingredients:**
    - In a medium bowl, whisk together flour, baking powder, baking soda, salt, and oats. Set aside.
3. **Cream Butter and Sugars:**
    - In a large bowl, use an electric mixer to cream together the butter, granulated sugar, and brown sugar until light and fluffy, about 3 minutes.
4. **Add Eggs and Vanilla:**
    - Beat in the eggs one at a time until fully incorporated. Mix in the vanilla extract.
5. **Combine Wet and Dry Ingredients:**
    - Gradually add the dry ingredients to the wet ingredients, mixing just until combined.
6. **Fold in Add-ins:**
    - Gently fold in the chocolate chips, chopped nuts, shredded coconut, and raisins or dried cranberries (if using) until evenly distributed throughout the dough.
7. **Form Cookies:**
    - Using a cookie scoop or tablespoon, drop rounded balls of dough onto the prepared baking sheets, spacing them about 2 inches apart.

8. **Bake:**
   - Bake in the preheated oven for 12-15 minutes, or until the edges are lightly golden and the centers are set but still soft.
9. **Cool:**
   - Allow the cookies to cool on the baking sheets for about 5 minutes before transferring them to a wire rack to cool completely.

Tips:

- **Butter Temperature:** Ensure the butter is at room temperature for the best mixing and cookie texture.
- **Mix-ins:** Feel free to adjust the mix-ins to your taste. You can substitute or omit ingredients based on what you have on hand or your personal preference.
- **Cookie Size:** For uniform cookies, use a cookie scoop or tablespoon to portion out the dough.

Enjoy your homemade Cowboy Cookies! They're a great way to use up various pantry ingredients and offer a satisfying, crunchy, and chewy treat.

Pumpkin Spice Cookies

Ingredients:

- **Dry Ingredients:**
    - 2 1/2 cups all-purpose flour
    - 1 teaspoon baking soda
    - 1/2 teaspoon baking powder
    - 1/2 teaspoon salt
    - 1 tablespoon ground cinnamon
    - 1/2 teaspoon ground ginger
    - 1/4 teaspoon ground nutmeg
    - 1/4 teaspoon ground cloves
- **Wet Ingredients:**
    - 1 cup (2 sticks) unsalted butter, room temperature
    - 1 cup granulated sugar
    - 1 cup packed brown sugar
    - 1 large egg
    - 1 cup canned pumpkin puree (not pumpkin pie filling)
    - 1 teaspoon vanilla extract
- **Optional Add-ins:**
    - 1/2 cup chopped nuts (such as walnuts or pecans)
    - 1/2 cup white chocolate chips or semisweet chocolate chips

Instructions:

1. **Preheat Oven:**
    - Preheat your oven to 350°F (175°C). Line baking sheets with parchment paper or silicone baking mats.
2. **Mix Dry Ingredients:**
    - In a medium bowl, whisk together flour, baking soda, baking powder, salt, cinnamon, ginger, nutmeg, and cloves. Set aside.
3. **Cream Butter and Sugars:**
    - In a large bowl, use an electric mixer to cream together the butter, granulated sugar, and brown sugar until light and fluffy, about 3 minutes.
4. **Add Egg, Pumpkin, and Vanilla:**
    - Beat in the egg until fully incorporated. Mix in the pumpkin puree and vanilla extract.
5. **Combine Wet and Dry Ingredients:**
    - Gradually add the dry ingredients to the wet ingredients, mixing just until combined.
6. **Fold in Add-ins (Optional):**
    - If using, gently fold in the chopped nuts and/or chocolate chips until evenly distributed throughout the dough.

7. **Form Cookies:**
   - Using a cookie scoop or tablespoon, drop rounded balls of dough onto the prepared baking sheets, spacing them about 2 inches apart.
8. **Bake:**
   - Bake in the preheated oven for 12-15 minutes, or until the edges are set and the centers are soft but no longer wet. The cookies should be golden around the edges.
9. **Cool:**
   - Allow the cookies to cool on the baking sheets for about 5 minutes before transferring them to a wire rack to cool completely.

Tips:

- **Pumpkin Puree:** Use pure pumpkin puree, not pumpkin pie filling, which contains added spices and sugars.
- **Spices:** Adjust the spices according to your taste. You can increase or decrease the amounts of cinnamon, ginger, nutmeg, and cloves as desired.
- **Texture:** These cookies are meant to be soft and cakey. Don't overbake them; they should remain moist in the center.

Enjoy your homemade Pumpkin Spice Cookies! They're a cozy and flavorful treat that captures the essence of fall in every bite.

Molasses Cookies

Ingredients:

- **Dry Ingredients:**
    - 2 1/4 cups all-purpose flour
    - 1/2 teaspoon baking soda
    - 1/2 teaspoon baking powder
    - 1/4 teaspoon salt
    - 1 tablespoon ground ginger
    - 1 teaspoon ground cinnamon
    - 1/4 teaspoon ground cloves
- **Wet Ingredients:**
    - 3/4 cup (1 1/2 sticks) unsalted butter, room temperature
    - 1 cup granulated sugar, plus extra for rolling
    - 1/2 cup packed brown sugar
    - 1 large egg
    - 1/2 cup molasses (unsulfured)

Instructions:

1. **Preheat Oven:**
    - Preheat your oven to 350°F (175°C). Line baking sheets with parchment paper or silicone baking mats.
2. **Mix Dry Ingredients:**
    - In a medium bowl, whisk together flour, baking soda, baking powder, salt, ginger, cinnamon, and cloves. Set aside.
3. **Cream Butter and Sugars:**
    - In a large bowl, use an electric mixer to cream together the butter, granulated sugar, and brown sugar until light and fluffy, about 3 minutes.
4. **Add Egg and Molasses:**
    - Beat in the egg until fully incorporated. Mix in the molasses until well combined.
5. **Combine Wet and Dry Ingredients:**
    - Gradually add the dry ingredients to the wet ingredients, mixing just until combined. Do not overmix.
6. **Form Cookies:**
    - Roll tablespoon-sized balls of dough in granulated sugar and place them onto the prepared baking sheets, spacing them about 2 inches apart. Flatten each ball slightly with the bottom of a glass or your fingers.
7. **Bake:**
    - Bake in the preheated oven for 10-12 minutes, or until the edges are set and the centers are soft. The cookies will continue to firm up as they cool.
8. **Cool:**

- Allow the cookies to cool on the baking sheets for about 5 minutes before transferring them to a wire rack to cool completely.

Tips:

- **Molasses:** Use unsulfured molasses for a milder flavor. Blackstrap molasses can be used for a stronger, more robust taste.
- **Rolling in Sugar:** Rolling the dough balls in granulated sugar before baking gives the cookies a nice, slightly crunchy exterior.
- **Storage:** Store cookies in an airtight container at room temperature for up to a week. They can also be frozen for longer storage.

Enjoy your homemade Molasses Cookies! They're perfect with a cup of tea or coffee and bring a comforting, spiced flavor to any occasion.

Nutella-Stuffed Cookies

Ingredients:

- **Dry Ingredients:**
    - 2 1/4 cups all-purpose flour
    - 1/2 teaspoon baking soda
    - 1/2 teaspoon baking powder
    - 1/4 teaspoon salt
- **Wet Ingredients:**
    - 1 cup (2 sticks) unsalted butter, room temperature
    - 1 cup granulated sugar
    - 1 cup packed brown sugar
    - 2 large eggs
    - 1 teaspoon vanilla extract
- **Add-ins:**
    - 1 cup semisweet chocolate chips
    - 1/2 cup Nutella (or other chocolate hazelnut spread)

Instructions:

1. **Preheat Oven:**
    - Preheat your oven to 350°F (175°C). Line baking sheets with parchment paper or silicone baking mats.
2. **Prepare Nutella:**
    - Scoop small amounts of Nutella (about 1/2 teaspoon each) onto a parchment-lined tray or plate. Freeze for at least 30 minutes to firm up. This will make it easier to stuff into the cookie dough.
3. **Mix Dry Ingredients:**
    - In a medium bowl, whisk together flour, baking soda, baking powder, and salt. Set aside.
4. **Cream Butter and Sugars:**
    - In a large bowl, use an electric mixer to cream together the butter, granulated sugar, and brown sugar until light and fluffy, about 3 minutes.
5. **Add Eggs and Vanilla:**
    - Beat in the eggs one at a time until fully incorporated. Mix in the vanilla extract.
6. **Combine Wet and Dry Ingredients:**
    - Gradually add the dry ingredients to the wet ingredients, mixing just until combined.
7. **Fold in Chocolate Chips:**
    - Gently fold in the chocolate chips until evenly distributed throughout the dough.
8. **Form Cookies:**
    - For each cookie, take a small amount of dough and flatten it into a disk. Place a frozen dollop of Nutella in the center and wrap the dough around it, pinching the

edges to seal. Roll the dough ball between your hands to smooth it out. Place on the prepared baking sheets, spacing them about 2 inches apart.

9. **Bake:**
   - Bake in the preheated oven for 12-15 minutes, or until the edges are lightly golden and the centers are set. The cookies may appear slightly underbaked in the center, which is okay; this helps keep the Nutella gooey.
10. **Cool:**
    - Allow the cookies to cool on the baking sheets for about 5 minutes before transferring them to a wire rack to cool completely.

Tips:

- **Chilling Nutella:** Freezing the Nutella makes it easier to handle and helps prevent it from melting too much during baking.
- **Dough Handling:** Be gentle when wrapping the dough around the Nutella to avoid breaking it open. If the dough is too sticky, you can chill it briefly before working with it.
- **Storage:** Store cookies in an airtight container at room temperature for up to a week. They can also be frozen for longer storage.

Enjoy your homemade Nutella-Stuffed Cookies! They're a delightful treat with a gooey, chocolatey surprise in every bite.

Caramel Apple Cookies

Ingredients:

- **Dry Ingredients:**
    - 2 1/4 cups all-purpose flour
    - 1/2 teaspoon baking soda
    - 1/2 teaspoon baking powder
    - 1/4 teaspoon salt
    - 1 teaspoon ground cinnamon
    - 1/4 teaspoon ground nutmeg
- **Wet Ingredients:**
    - 1 cup (2 sticks) unsalted butter, room temperature
    - 1 cup granulated sugar
    - 1 cup packed brown sugar
    - 2 large eggs
    - 1 teaspoon vanilla extract
- **Add-ins:**
    - 1 1/2 cups diced apple (peeled and cored)
    - 1/2 cup caramel bits or chopped caramel candies
    - 1/2 cup chopped nuts (optional, such as pecans or walnuts)

Instructions:

1. **Preheat Oven:**
    - Preheat your oven to 350°F (175°C). Line baking sheets with parchment paper or silicone baking mats.
2. **Mix Dry Ingredients:**
    - In a medium bowl, whisk together flour, baking soda, baking powder, salt, cinnamon, and nutmeg. Set aside.
3. **Cream Butter and Sugars:**
    - In a large bowl, use an electric mixer to cream together the butter, granulated sugar, and brown sugar until light and fluffy, about 3 minutes.
4. **Add Eggs and Vanilla:**
    - Beat in the eggs one at a time until fully incorporated. Mix in the vanilla extract.
5. **Combine Wet and Dry Ingredients:**
    - Gradually add the dry ingredients to the wet ingredients, mixing just until combined.
6. **Fold in Add-ins:**
    - Gently fold in the diced apple, caramel bits, and chopped nuts (if using) until evenly distributed throughout the dough.
7. **Form Cookies:**
    - Using a cookie scoop or tablespoon, drop rounded balls of dough onto the prepared baking sheets, spacing them about 2 inches apart.

8. **Bake:**
   - Bake in the preheated oven for 12-15 minutes, or until the edges are lightly golden and the centers are set. The cookies may appear soft, which is fine; they will firm up as they cool.
9. **Cool:**
   - Allow the cookies to cool on the baking sheets for about 5 minutes before transferring them to a wire rack to cool completely.

Tips:

- **Apples:** Use firm apples that hold their shape well during baking, such as Granny Smith or Honeycrisp. Dice them into small, bite-sized pieces to ensure they mix evenly into the dough.
- **Caramel Bits:** You can use pre-packaged caramel bits or chop up caramel candies. If using caramel candies, ensure they are chopped into small pieces.
- **Nuts:** Nuts are optional, but they add a nice crunch and extra flavor. Toast them lightly before adding if you want to enhance their flavor.

Enjoy your homemade Caramel Apple Cookies! They're a delightful blend of sweet and fruity with a touch of caramel that's sure to satisfy your cravings.

Raspberry Jam Thumbprint Cookies

Ingredients:

- **Dry Ingredients:**
    - 1 3/4 cups all-purpose flour
    - 1/4 teaspoon salt
    - 1/4 teaspoon baking powder
- **Wet Ingredients:**
    - 1/2 cup (1 stick) unsalted butter, room temperature
    - 1/2 cup granulated sugar
    - 1 large egg yolk
    - 1 teaspoon vanilla extract
- **For Filling:**
    - 1/2 cup raspberry jam or preserves
- **For Rolling:**
    - 1/4 cup granulated sugar (optional)

Instructions:

1. **Preheat Oven:**
    - Preheat your oven to 350°F (175°C). Line baking sheets with parchment paper or silicone baking mats.
2. **Mix Dry Ingredients:**
    - In a medium bowl, whisk together flour, salt, and baking powder. Set aside.
3. **Cream Butter and Sugar:**
    - In a large bowl, use an electric mixer to cream together the butter and granulated sugar until light and fluffy, about 2-3 minutes.
4. **Add Egg Yolk and Vanilla:**
    - Beat in the egg yolk until fully incorporated. Mix in the vanilla extract.
5. **Combine Wet and Dry Ingredients:**
    - Gradually add the dry ingredients to the wet ingredients, mixing just until combined. The dough will be thick and slightly crumbly.
6. **Form Cookies:**
    - Roll the dough into 1-inch balls and place them on the prepared baking sheets. Use your thumb or the back of a small spoon to make an indentation in the center of each ball.
7. **Add Jam:**
    - Spoon a small amount of raspberry jam into each indentation, being careful not to overfill.
8. **Optional Rolling:**
    - If desired, roll the dough balls in granulated sugar before placing them on the baking sheets for an extra touch of sweetness.
9. **Bake:**

- Bake in the preheated oven for 10-12 minutes, or until the edges are lightly golden. The jam may bubble slightly during baking.
10. **Cool:**
    - Allow the cookies to cool on the baking sheets for about 5 minutes before transferring them to a wire rack to cool completely.

Tips:

- **Jam:** Use a high-quality raspberry jam or preserves for the best flavor. You can also substitute with other flavors like strawberry or apricot if desired.
- **Dough Consistency:** If the dough is too crumbly to form balls, add a teaspoon of milk to help bind it together.
- **Indentations:** Be sure to make a deep enough indentation to hold the jam, but not so deep that the cookies fall apart.

Enjoy your homemade Raspberry Jam Thumbprint Cookies! They're a delightful combination of buttery cookie and sweet, tangy raspberry filling, perfect for any cookie tray or as a treat for yourself.

Espresso Cookies

Ingredients:

- **Dry Ingredients:**
    - 2 1/4 cups all-purpose flour
    - 1/2 teaspoon baking soda
    - 1/2 teaspoon baking powder
    - 1/4 teaspoon salt
    - 1 tablespoon instant espresso powder or finely ground espresso beans
- **Wet Ingredients:**
    - 1 cup (2 sticks) unsalted butter, room temperature
    - 1 cup granulated sugar
    - 1 cup packed brown sugar
    - 2 large eggs
    - 1 teaspoon vanilla extract
- **Add-ins:**
    - 1 cup semisweet chocolate chips or chunks
    - 1/2 cup chopped nuts (optional, such as walnuts or pecans)

Instructions:

1. **Preheat Oven:**
    - Preheat your oven to 350°F (175°C). Line baking sheets with parchment paper or silicone baking mats.
2. **Mix Dry Ingredients:**
    - In a medium bowl, whisk together flour, baking soda, baking powder, salt, and instant espresso powder. Set aside.
3. **Cream Butter and Sugars:**
    - In a large bowl, use an electric mixer to cream together the butter, granulated sugar, and brown sugar until light and fluffy, about 2-3 minutes.
4. **Add Eggs and Vanilla:**
    - Beat in the eggs one at a time until fully incorporated. Mix in the vanilla extract.
5. **Combine Wet and Dry Ingredients:**
    - Gradually add the dry ingredients to the wet ingredients, mixing just until combined. Be careful not to overmix.
6. **Fold in Add-ins:**
    - Gently fold in the chocolate chips and chopped nuts (if using) until evenly distributed throughout the dough.
7. **Form Cookies:**
    - Using a cookie scoop or tablespoon, drop rounded balls of dough onto the prepared baking sheets, spacing them about 2 inches apart.
8. **Bake:**

- Bake in the preheated oven for 10-12 minutes, or until the edges are lightly golden and the centers are set. The cookies may appear slightly underbaked in the center; this is okay.
9. **Cool:**
    - Allow the cookies to cool on the baking sheets for about 5 minutes before transferring them to a wire rack to cool completely.

Tips:

- **Espresso Powder:** For a stronger coffee flavor, you can increase the amount of espresso powder. Just be cautious not to overpower the cookies.
- **Instant Espresso Powder:** If you can't find instant espresso powder, you can use finely ground espresso beans, but make sure they are ground very fine to avoid a gritty texture.
- **Texture:** If the dough is too sticky to handle, you can chill it in the refrigerator for about 30 minutes before baking.

Enjoy your homemade Espresso Cookies! They're a great way to combine your love for coffee with a sweet treat, offering a delicious burst of espresso flavor in every bite.

Chocolate-Dipped Coconut Cookies

Ingredients:

- **For the Cookies:**
    - 1 1/2 cups all-purpose flour
    - 1/2 teaspoon baking powder
    - 1/4 teaspoon salt
    - 1/2 cup (1 stick) unsalted butter, room temperature
    - 1 cup granulated sugar
    - 1 large egg
    - 1 teaspoon vanilla extract
    - 1 1/2 cups sweetened shredded coconut
- **For the Chocolate Dip:**
    - 1 cup semisweet chocolate chips
    - 2 tablespoons coconut oil or vegetable oil (optional, for a smoother dip)

Instructions:

1. **Preheat Oven:**
    - Preheat your oven to 350°F (175°C). Line baking sheets with parchment paper or silicone baking mats.
2. **Mix Dry Ingredients:**
    - In a medium bowl, whisk together flour, baking powder, and salt. Set aside.
3. **Cream Butter and Sugar:**
    - In a large bowl, use an electric mixer to cream together the butter and granulated sugar until light and fluffy, about 2-3 minutes.
4. **Add Egg and Vanilla:**
    - Beat in the egg until fully incorporated. Mix in the vanilla extract.
5. **Combine Wet and Dry Ingredients:**
    - Gradually add the dry ingredients to the wet ingredients, mixing just until combined.
6. **Add Coconut:**
    - Gently fold in the shredded coconut until evenly distributed throughout the dough.
7. **Form Cookies:**
    - Using a cookie scoop or tablespoon, drop rounded balls of dough onto the prepared baking sheets, spacing them about 2 inches apart. Flatten each ball slightly with the back of a spoon or your fingers.
8. **Bake:**
    - Bake in the preheated oven for 10-12 minutes, or until the edges are lightly golden. The centers will be soft but will firm up as they cool.
9. **Cool:**
    - Allow the cookies to cool on the baking sheets for about 5 minutes before transferring them to a wire rack to cool completely.

10. **Prepare Chocolate Dip:**
    - In a microwave-safe bowl, melt the chocolate chips with the coconut oil or vegetable oil (if using) in 30-second intervals, stirring between each interval until smooth and fully melted.
11. **Dip Cookies:**
    - Dip the cooled cookies halfway into the melted chocolate, allowing the excess chocolate to drip off. Place the dipped cookies on a parchment-lined tray to set. You can also sprinkle extra shredded coconut on top of the chocolate before it sets, if desired.
12. **Set:**
    - Allow the chocolate to set completely before serving. You can speed up the process by placing the cookies in the refrigerator for about 15-20 minutes.

Tips:

- **Chocolate Coating:** Adding coconut oil or vegetable oil to the chocolate helps it to be more fluid and smooth, making it easier to coat the cookies.
- **Storage:** Store the cookies in an airtight container at room temperature for up to a week, or in the refrigerator for longer storage. They can also be frozen for up to 3 months.
- **Variation:** You can use dark chocolate or milk chocolate instead of semisweet, depending on your preference.

Enjoy your homemade Chocolate-Dipped Coconut Cookies! They're a delicious blend of chewy coconut and smooth chocolate, perfect for sharing or enjoying with a cup of coffee or tea.

S'mores Cookies

Ingredients:

- **Dry Ingredients:**
    - 1 3/4 cups all-purpose flour
    - 1/2 teaspoon baking soda
    - 1/4 teaspoon salt
- **Wet Ingredients:**
    - 1 cup (2 sticks) unsalted butter, room temperature
    - 1 cup granulated sugar
    - 1 cup packed brown sugar
    - 2 large eggs
    - 1 teaspoon vanilla extract
- **Add-ins:**
    - 1 cup semisweet chocolate chips or chunks
    - 1 cup mini marshmallows (or regular marshmallows, cut into small pieces)
    - 1 cup crushed graham crackers (about 6-8 graham cracker sheets)

Instructions:

1. **Preheat Oven:**
    - Preheat your oven to 350°F (175°C). Line baking sheets with parchment paper or silicone baking mats.
2. **Mix Dry Ingredients:**
    - In a medium bowl, whisk together flour, baking soda, and salt. Set aside.
3. **Cream Butter and Sugars:**
    - In a large bowl, use an electric mixer to cream together the butter, granulated sugar, and brown sugar until light and fluffy, about 2-3 minutes.
4. **Add Eggs and Vanilla:**
    - Beat in the eggs one at a time until fully incorporated. Mix in the vanilla extract.
5. **Combine Wet and Dry Ingredients:**
    - Gradually add the dry ingredients to the wet ingredients, mixing just until combined.
6. **Fold in Add-ins:**
    - Gently fold in the chocolate chips, mini marshmallows, and crushed graham crackers until evenly distributed throughout the dough. Be careful not to overmix.
7. **Form Cookies:**
    - Using a cookie scoop or tablespoon, drop rounded balls of dough onto the prepared baking sheets, spacing them about 2 inches apart. Flatten each ball slightly with the back of a spoon or your fingers.
8. **Bake:**

- Bake in the preheated oven for 10-12 minutes, or until the edges are lightly golden and the centers are just set. The marshmallows might puff up and slightly melt, which is fine.

9. **Cool:**
   - Allow the cookies to cool on the baking sheets for about 5 minutes before transferring them to a wire rack to cool completely. The marshmallows will firm up as they cool.

Tips:

- **Marshmallows:** If using large marshmallows, cut them into small pieces to ensure they distribute evenly throughout the dough.
- **Graham Crackers:** For a more intense graham cracker flavor, you can use graham cracker crumbs instead of crushed graham crackers.
- **Texture:** The cookies may appear soft in the center but will firm up as they cool. If you prefer a crispier cookie, bake them an additional 1-2 minutes.
- **Storage:** Store the cookies in an airtight container at room temperature for up to a week. They can also be frozen for up to 3 months.

Enjoy your homemade S'mores Cookies! They bring the nostalgic flavors of s'mores into a convenient, chewy cookie form, perfect for satisfying your sweet tooth or sharing with friends and family.

Pumpkin Oatmeal Cookies

Ingredients:

- **Dry Ingredients:**
    - 1 1/2 cups all-purpose flour
    - 1 teaspoon baking powder
    - 1/2 teaspoon baking soda
    - 1/2 teaspoon salt
    - 1 teaspoon ground cinnamon
    - 1/2 teaspoon ground nutmeg
    - 1/4 teaspoon ground ginger
    - 1/4 teaspoon ground cloves
- **Wet Ingredients:**
    - 1/2 cup (1 stick) unsalted butter, room temperature
    - 1/2 cup granulated sugar
    - 1/2 cup packed brown sugar
    - 1 large egg
    - 1 teaspoon vanilla extract
    - 1 cup canned pumpkin (not pumpkin pie filling)
- **Add-ins:**
    - 1 1/2 cups old-fashioned rolled oats
    - 1/2 cup chocolate chips or chopped nuts (optional)

Instructions:

1. **Preheat Oven:**
    - Preheat your oven to 350°F (175°C). Line baking sheets with parchment paper or silicone baking mats.
2. **Mix Dry Ingredients:**
    - In a medium bowl, whisk together flour, baking powder, baking soda, salt, cinnamon, nutmeg, ginger, and cloves. Set aside.
3. **Cream Butter and Sugars:**
    - In a large bowl, use an electric mixer to cream together the butter, granulated sugar, and brown sugar until light and fluffy, about 2-3 minutes.
4. **Add Egg, Vanilla, and Pumpkin:**
    - Beat in the egg until fully incorporated. Mix in the vanilla extract and canned pumpkin until smooth.
5. **Combine Wet and Dry Ingredients:**
    - Gradually add the dry ingredients to the wet ingredients, mixing just until combined.
6. **Fold in Oats and Optional Add-ins:**
    - Gently fold in the rolled oats and, if desired, chocolate chips or chopped nuts until evenly distributed throughout the dough.

7. **Form Cookies:**
   - Using a cookie scoop or tablespoon, drop rounded balls of dough onto the prepared baking sheets, spacing them about 2 inches apart. Flatten each ball slightly with the back of a spoon or your fingers.
8. **Bake:**
   - Bake in the preheated oven for 10-12 minutes, or until the edges are lightly golden and the centers are set. The cookies will be soft but will firm up as they cool.
9. **Cool:**
   - Allow the cookies to cool on the baking sheets for about 5 minutes before transferring them to a wire rack to cool completely.

Tips:

- **Pumpkin:** Make sure to use pure canned pumpkin, not pumpkin pie filling, to avoid extra sugars and spices.
- **Texture:** These cookies may appear soft in the center when they come out of the oven. They will firm up as they cool.
- **Oats:** Old-fashioned rolled oats work best for texture. Quick oats can be used but may result in a softer texture.
- **Storage:** Store the cookies in an airtight container at room temperature for up to a week, or freeze for longer storage.

Enjoy your homemade Pumpkin Oatmeal Cookies! They're a perfect blend of cozy fall flavors and the satisfying chewiness of oatmeal, ideal for any autumn day or holiday gathering.

Chai Spice Cookies

Ingredients:

- **Dry Ingredients:**
    - 2 1/4 cups all-purpose flour
    - 1/2 teaspoon baking soda
    - 1/2 teaspoon baking powder
    - 1/4 teaspoon salt
    - 1 teaspoon ground cinnamon
    - 1/2 teaspoon ground ginger
    - 1/2 teaspoon ground cardamom
    - 1/4 teaspoon ground cloves
    - 1/4 teaspoon ground black pepper (optional, for a hint of heat)
- **Wet Ingredients:**
    - 1 cup (2 sticks) unsalted butter, room temperature
    - 1 cup granulated sugar
    - 1/2 cup packed brown sugar
    - 1 large egg
    - 1 teaspoon vanilla extract
- **For Rolling:**
    - 1/4 cup granulated sugar (optional, for rolling)

Instructions:

1. **Preheat Oven:**
    - Preheat your oven to 350°F (175°C). Line baking sheets with parchment paper or silicone baking mats.
2. **Mix Dry Ingredients:**
    - In a medium bowl, whisk together flour, baking soda, baking powder, salt, cinnamon, ginger, cardamom, cloves, and black pepper (if using). Set aside.
3. **Cream Butter and Sugars:**
    - In a large bowl, use an electric mixer to cream together the butter, granulated sugar, and brown sugar until light and fluffy, about 2-3 minutes.
4. **Add Egg and Vanilla:**
    - Beat in the egg until fully incorporated. Mix in the vanilla extract.
5. **Combine Wet and Dry Ingredients:**
    - Gradually add the dry ingredients to the wet ingredients, mixing just until combined.
6. **Form Cookies:**
    - Using a cookie scoop or tablespoon, drop rounded balls of dough onto the prepared baking sheets, spacing them about 2 inches apart. If desired, roll the dough balls in granulated sugar before placing them on the baking sheets for extra sweetness and a bit of crunch.

7. **Bake:**
   - Bake in the preheated oven for 10-12 minutes, or until the edges are lightly golden. The centers will be soft but will firm up as they cool.
8. **Cool:**
   - Allow the cookies to cool on the baking sheets for about 5 minutes before transferring them to a wire rack to cool completely.

Tips:

- **Spice Blend:** Adjust the spices to your taste. If you prefer a spicier cookie, you can add a bit more ginger or cardamom.
- **Texture:** These cookies will be soft and chewy. For a crisper cookie, bake them a minute or two longer.
- **Storage:** Store the cookies in an airtight container at room temperature for up to a week, or freeze for longer storage.

Enjoy your homemade Chai Spice Cookies! They offer a comforting mix of spices and sweetness, making them a perfect treat for any time you want to indulge in something warm and flavorful.

Cranberry White Chocolate Cookies

Ingredients:

- **Dry Ingredients:**
    - 2 1/4 cups all-purpose flour
    - 1/2 teaspoon baking soda
    - 1/2 teaspoon baking powder
    - 1/4 teaspoon salt
- **Wet Ingredients:**
    - 1 cup (2 sticks) unsalted butter, room temperature
    - 1 cup granulated sugar
    - 1 cup packed brown sugar
    - 2 large eggs
    - 1 teaspoon vanilla extract
- **Add-ins:**
    - 1 cup dried cranberries
    - 1 cup white chocolate chips or chopped white chocolate

Instructions:

1. **Preheat Oven:**
    - Preheat your oven to 350°F (175°C). Line baking sheets with parchment paper or silicone baking mats.
2. **Mix Dry Ingredients:**
    - In a medium bowl, whisk together flour, baking soda, baking powder, and salt. Set aside.
3. **Cream Butter and Sugars:**
    - In a large bowl, use an electric mixer to cream together the butter, granulated sugar, and brown sugar until light and fluffy, about 2-3 minutes.
4. **Add Eggs and Vanilla:**
    - Beat in the eggs one at a time until fully incorporated. Mix in the vanilla extract.
5. **Combine Wet and Dry Ingredients:**
    - Gradually add the dry ingredients to the wet ingredients, mixing just until combined.
6. **Fold in Add-ins:**
    - Gently fold in the dried cranberries and white chocolate chips until evenly distributed throughout the dough.
7. **Form Cookies:**
    - Using a cookie scoop or tablespoon, drop rounded balls of dough onto the prepared baking sheets, spacing them about 2 inches apart.
8. **Bake:**

- Bake in the preheated oven for 10-12 minutes, or until the edges are lightly golden and the centers are set. The cookies will be soft but will firm up as they cool.

9. **Cool:**
    - Allow the cookies to cool on the baking sheets for about 5 minutes before transferring them to a wire rack to cool completely.

Tips:

- **Cranberries:** If using large dried cranberries, consider chopping them into smaller pieces to ensure they distribute evenly throughout the dough.
- **White Chocolate:** You can use white chocolate chips or chop a bar of white chocolate into chunks, depending on your preference.
- **Storage:** Store the cookies in an airtight container at room temperature for up to a week, or freeze for longer storage.

Enjoy your homemade Cranberry White Chocolate Cookies! They're a perfect combination of tart and sweet, making them a delightful treat for any occasion, especially during the holidays.

Maple Pecan Cookies

Ingredients:

- **Dry Ingredients:**
    - 2 cups all-purpose flour
    - 1/2 teaspoon baking soda
    - 1/2 teaspoon baking powder
    - 1/4 teaspoon salt
- **Wet Ingredients:**
    - 1 cup (2 sticks) unsalted butter, room temperature
    - 1 cup granulated sugar
    - 1/2 cup packed brown sugar
    - 1 large egg
    - 1/2 cup pure maple syrup (not imitation maple syrup)
    - 1 teaspoon vanilla extract
- **Add-ins:**
    - 1 cup chopped pecans (toasted if desired)

Instructions:

1. **Preheat Oven:**
    - Preheat your oven to 350°F (175°C). Line baking sheets with parchment paper or silicone baking mats.
2. **Mix Dry Ingredients:**
    - In a medium bowl, whisk together flour, baking soda, baking powder, and salt. Set aside.
3. **Cream Butter and Sugars:**
    - In a large bowl, use an electric mixer to cream together the butter, granulated sugar, and brown sugar until light and fluffy, about 2-3 minutes.
4. **Add Egg, Maple Syrup, and Vanilla:**
    - Beat in the egg until fully incorporated. Mix in the maple syrup and vanilla extract until smooth.
5. **Combine Wet and Dry Ingredients:**
    - Gradually add the dry ingredients to the wet ingredients, mixing just until combined.
6. **Fold in Pecans:**
    - Gently fold in the chopped pecans until evenly distributed throughout the dough.
7. **Form Cookies:**
    - Using a cookie scoop or tablespoon, drop rounded balls of dough onto the prepared baking sheets, spacing them about 2 inches apart. Flatten each ball slightly with the back of a spoon or your fingers.
8. **Bake:**

- Bake in the preheated oven for 10-12 minutes, or until the edges are lightly golden and the centers are set. The cookies will be soft but will firm up as they cool.
9. **Cool:**
   - Allow the cookies to cool on the baking sheets for about 5 minutes before transferring them to a wire rack to cool completely.

Tips:

- **Maple Syrup:** Use pure maple syrup for the best flavor. Imitation maple syrup will not provide the same depth of taste.
- **Pecans:** Toasting the pecans before chopping can enhance their flavor. To toast, place them in a single layer on a baking sheet and bake at 350°F (175°C) for about 5-7 minutes, or until fragrant. Let cool before adding to the dough.
- **Storage:** Store the cookies in an airtight container at room temperature for up to a week, or freeze for longer storage.

Enjoy your homemade Maple Pecan Cookies! They offer a delightful combination of sweet maple syrup and crunchy pecans, making them a perfect treat for any occasion.

Peanut Butter Blossoms

Ingredients:

- **For the Cookies:**
    - 1 3/4 cups all-purpose flour
    - 1/2 teaspoon baking soda
    - 1/2 teaspoon baking powder
    - 1/4 teaspoon salt
    - 1/2 cup (1 stick) unsalted butter, room temperature
    - 1/2 cup granulated sugar
    - 1/2 cup packed brown sugar
    - 1/2 cup creamy peanut butter
    - 1 large egg
    - 1 teaspoon vanilla extract
- **For Rolling:**
    - 1/4 cup granulated sugar
- **For Topping:**
    - 36 Hershey's Kisses or other chocolate candies (unwrapped)

Instructions:

1. **Preheat Oven:**
    - Preheat your oven to 350°F (175°C). Line baking sheets with parchment paper or silicone baking mats.
2. **Mix Dry Ingredients:**
    - In a medium bowl, whisk together flour, baking soda, baking powder, and salt. Set aside.
3. **Cream Butter and Sugars:**
    - In a large bowl, use an electric mixer to cream together the butter, granulated sugar, and brown sugar until light and fluffy, about 2-3 minutes.
4. **Add Peanut Butter, Egg, and Vanilla:**
    - Beat in the peanut butter until well combined. Mix in the egg and vanilla extract until smooth.
5. **Combine Wet and Dry Ingredients:**
    - Gradually add the dry ingredients to the wet ingredients, mixing just until combined.
6. **Form Cookies:**
    - Roll rounded tablespoonfuls of dough into balls. Roll each ball in granulated sugar to coat, then place them on the prepared baking sheets, spacing them about 2 inches apart.
7. **Bake:**
    - Bake in the preheated oven for 8-10 minutes, or until the edges are set and the cookies are lightly golden.

8. **Add Kisses:**
    - Remove the cookies from the oven and immediately press a Hershey's Kiss into the center of each cookie. The cookie will slightly crack around the edges.
9. **Cool:**
    - Allow the cookies to cool on the baking sheets for about 5 minutes before transferring them to a wire rack to cool completely.

Tips:

- **Peanut Butter:** Use creamy peanut butter for a smoother texture. If using natural peanut butter, ensure it's well-stirred before measuring.
- **Chocolate Kisses:** For a different flavor, try using other types of chocolate or candy melts in place of the Hershey's Kisses.
- **Storage:** Store the cookies in an airtight container at room temperature for up to a week, or freeze for longer storage.

Enjoy your homemade Peanut Butter Blossoms! They're a delicious combination of rich peanut butter and sweet chocolate, making them a hit at any gathering or as a treat for yourself.

Butterfinger Cookies

Ingredients:

- **Dry Ingredients:**
    - 1 3/4 cups all-purpose flour
    - 1/2 teaspoon baking soda
    - 1/2 teaspoon baking powder
    - 1/4 teaspoon salt
- **Wet Ingredients:**
    - 1 cup (2 sticks) unsalted butter, room temperature
    - 1 cup granulated sugar
    - 1/2 cup packed brown sugar
    - 1 large egg
    - 1 teaspoon vanilla extract
- **Add-ins:**
    - 1 cup chopped Butterfinger bars (about 4-5 bars)
    - 1/2 cup chocolate chips (optional)

Instructions:

1. **Preheat Oven:**
    - Preheat your oven to 350°F (175°C). Line baking sheets with parchment paper or silicone baking mats.
2. **Mix Dry Ingredients:**
    - In a medium bowl, whisk together flour, baking soda, baking powder, and salt. Set aside.
3. **Cream Butter and Sugars:**
    - In a large bowl, use an electric mixer to cream together the butter, granulated sugar, and brown sugar until light and fluffy, about 2-3 minutes.
4. **Add Egg and Vanilla:**
    - Beat in the egg until fully incorporated. Mix in the vanilla extract.
5. **Combine Wet and Dry Ingredients:**
    - Gradually add the dry ingredients to the wet ingredients, mixing just until combined.
6. **Fold in Butterfingers and Optional Chocolate Chips:**
    - Gently fold in the chopped Butterfinger bars and chocolate chips (if using) until evenly distributed throughout the dough.
7. **Form Cookies:**
    - Using a cookie scoop or tablespoon, drop rounded balls of dough onto the prepared baking sheets, spacing them about 2 inches apart.
8. **Bake:**

- Bake in the preheated oven for 10-12 minutes, or until the edges are lightly golden and the centers are set. The cookies will be soft but will firm up as they cool.
9. **Cool:**
    - Allow the cookies to cool on the baking sheets for about 5 minutes before transferring them to a wire rack to cool completely.

Tips:

- **Butterfinger Bars:** Chop the Butterfinger bars into small pieces to ensure they distribute evenly throughout the dough and don't become too large in the cookies.
- **Texture:** These cookies will be chewy with crunchy bits of Butterfinger throughout. For a softer cookie, avoid overbaking.
- **Storage:** Store the cookies in an airtight container at room temperature for up to a week, or freeze for longer storage.

Enjoy your homemade Butterfinger Cookies! They offer a delightful crunch and peanut butter flavor that makes them a tasty and unique treat.

Cheesecake Cookies

Ingredients:

- **For the Cookies:**
    - 2 1/4 cups all-purpose flour
    - 1/2 teaspoon baking soda
    - 1/2 teaspoon baking powder
    - 1/4 teaspoon salt
- **For the Cream Cheese Filling:**
    - 4 oz (1/2 cup) cream cheese, softened
    - 1/4 cup granulated sugar
    - 1/4 teaspoon vanilla extract
    - 1 tablespoon all-purpose flour
- **For the Cookie Dough:**
    - 1 cup (2 sticks) unsalted butter, room temperature
    - 1 cup granulated sugar
    - 1/2 cup packed brown sugar
    - 1 large egg
    - 1 teaspoon vanilla extract

Instructions:

1. **Preheat Oven:**
    - Preheat your oven to 350°F (175°C). Line baking sheets with parchment paper or silicone baking mats.
2. **Prepare Cream Cheese Filling:**
    - In a small bowl, beat together the softened cream cheese, granulated sugar, vanilla extract, and flour until smooth. Set aside.
3. **Mix Dry Ingredients:**
    - In a medium bowl, whisk together flour, baking soda, baking powder, and salt. Set aside.
4. **Cream Butter and Sugars:**
    - In a large bowl, use an electric mixer to cream together the butter, granulated sugar, and brown sugar until light and fluffy, about 2-3 minutes.
5. **Add Egg and Vanilla:**
    - Beat in the egg until fully incorporated. Mix in the vanilla extract.
6. **Combine Wet and Dry Ingredients:**
    - Gradually add the dry ingredients to the wet ingredients, mixing just until combined.
7. **Form Cookies:**
    - Using a cookie scoop or tablespoon, drop rounded balls of dough onto the prepared baking sheets, spacing them about 2 inches apart.
8. **Add Cream Cheese Filling:**

- Make a small indentation in the center of each cookie dough ball with your thumb or the back of a spoon. Spoon a small amount of the cream cheese filling into each indentation.
9. **Bake:**
    - Bake in the preheated oven for 12-15 minutes, or until the edges are lightly golden and the centers are set. The cream cheese filling will be soft and slightly puffed.
10. **Cool:**
    - Allow the cookies to cool on the baking sheets for about 5 minutes before transferring them to a wire rack to cool completely.

Tips:

- **Cream Cheese:** Ensure the cream cheese is fully softened to avoid lumps in the filling. You can use a hand mixer or stand mixer to beat the filling until smooth.
- **Texture:** The cookies will be soft with a creamy filling in the center. Be careful not to overbake them.
- **Storage:** Store the cookies in an airtight container in the refrigerator for up to a week, or freeze for longer storage.

Enjoy your homemade Cheesecake Cookies! They offer a delightful blend of cheesecake creaminess and cookie comfort, making them a unique and delicious treat.

Brookie Cookies (Brownie-Cookie Hybrid)

Ingredients:

- **For the Brownie Layer:**
    - 1/2 cup (1 stick) unsalted butter
    - 1 cup granulated sugar
    - 2 large eggs
    - 1 teaspoon vanilla extract
    - 1/3 cup unsweetened cocoa powder
    - 1/2 cup all-purpose flour
    - 1/4 teaspoon salt
    - 1/4 teaspoon baking powder
    - 1/2 cup chocolate chips or chunks (optional)
- **For the Cookie Layer:**
    - 1/2 cup (1 stick) unsalted butter, room temperature
    - 1/2 cup granulated sugar
    - 1/2 cup packed brown sugar
    - 1 large egg
    - 1 teaspoon vanilla extract
    - 1 1/2 cups all-purpose flour
    - 1/2 teaspoon baking soda
    - 1/4 teaspoon salt
    - 1/2 cup chocolate chips

Instructions:

1. **Preheat Oven:**
    - Preheat your oven to 350°F (175°C). Line baking sheets with parchment paper or silicone baking mats.
2. **Prepare Brownie Layer:**
    - In a medium saucepan over low heat, melt the butter. Remove from heat and stir in granulated sugar, eggs, and vanilla extract. Mix in cocoa powder, flour, salt, and baking powder until just combined. Stir in chocolate chips or chunks if using. Set aside.
3. **Prepare Cookie Layer:**
    - In a large bowl, use an electric mixer to cream together the butter, granulated sugar, and brown sugar until light and fluffy. Beat in the egg and vanilla extract until smooth.
    - In a separate bowl, whisk together flour, baking soda, and salt. Gradually add the dry ingredients to the wet ingredients, mixing just until combined. Stir in chocolate chips.
4. **Assemble Brookies:**

- Using a cookie scoop or tablespoon, drop a spoonful of cookie dough onto the prepared baking sheets. Follow with a spoonful of brownie batter on top of the cookie dough. You can use a toothpick or knife to swirl the brownie and cookie dough together slightly for a marbled effect.

5. **Bake:**
   - Bake in the preheated oven for 10-12 minutes, or until the edges are set and the tops are slightly cracked. The centers will still be soft but will firm up as they cool.

6. **Cool:**
   - Allow the cookies to cool on the baking sheets for about 5 minutes before transferring them to a wire rack to cool completely.

Tips:

- **Swirling:** For a marbled look, be careful not to overmix the brownie and cookie layers. Swirl gently with a toothpick or knife.
- **Texture:** These cookies will have a rich, fudgy center with a slightly crisp edge. Be cautious not to overbake them to keep the brownie layer soft.
- **Storage:** Store the cookies in an airtight container at room temperature for up to a week, or freeze for longer storage.

Enjoy your homemade Brookie Cookies! They offer the perfect combination of chewy cookie and fudgy brownie, making them a decadent and irresistible treat.

Sea Salt Caramel Cookies

Ingredients:

- **For the Cookies:**
    - 1 3/4 cups all-purpose flour
    - 1/2 teaspoon baking soda
    - 1/4 teaspoon salt
- **For the Cookie Dough:**
    - 1 cup (2 sticks) unsalted butter, room temperature
    - 1 cup granulated sugar
    - 1/2 cup packed brown sugar
    - 1 large egg
    - 1 teaspoon vanilla extract
- **For the Caramel Filling:**
    - 1 cup caramel bits or soft caramel candies (unwrapped)
    - 2 tablespoons heavy cream
- **For Topping:**
    - Sea salt (for sprinkling)

Instructions:

1. **Prepare Caramel Filling:**
    - In a microwave-safe bowl or using a double boiler, melt the caramel bits with the heavy cream. Stir until smooth. Let the caramel cool slightly but keep it warm enough to be spooned or piped.
2. **Preheat Oven:**
    - Preheat your oven to 350°F (175°C). Line baking sheets with parchment paper or silicone baking mats.
3. **Mix Dry Ingredients:**
    - In a medium bowl, whisk together flour, baking soda, and salt. Set aside.
4. **Cream Butter and Sugars:**
    - In a large bowl, use an electric mixer to cream together the butter, granulated sugar, and brown sugar until light and fluffy, about 2-3 minutes.
5. **Add Egg and Vanilla:**
    - Beat in the egg until fully incorporated. Mix in the vanilla extract until smooth.
6. **Combine Wet and Dry Ingredients:**
    - Gradually add the dry ingredients to the wet ingredients, mixing just until combined.
7. **Form Cookies:**
    - Using a cookie scoop or tablespoon, drop rounded balls of dough onto the prepared baking sheets, spacing them about 2 inches apart. Flatten each ball slightly with the back of a spoon.
8. **Add Caramel Filling:**

- Make a small indentation in the center of each cookie dough ball with your thumb or the back of a spoon. Spoon a small amount of the warm caramel into each indentation.

9. **Bake:**
   - Bake in the preheated oven for 10-12 minutes, or until the edges are lightly golden and the cookies are set. The caramel will bubble slightly but should stay contained in the cookie.
10. **Add Sea Salt:**
    - As soon as the cookies come out of the oven, sprinkle a small pinch of sea salt on top of each caramel-filled cookie while still warm.
11. **Cool:**
    - Allow the cookies to cool on the baking sheets for about 5 minutes before transferring them to a wire rack to cool completely.

Tips:

- **Caramel:** If the caramel thickens too much while cooling, you can gently reheat it to make it easier to work with.
- **Sea Salt:** Use a coarse sea salt for a nice crunch and burst of flavor. Adjust the amount to your taste.
- **Storage:** Store the cookies in an airtight container at room temperature for up to a week. They can also be frozen for longer storage.

Enjoy your homemade Sea Salt Caramel Cookies! The combination of sweet caramel and a touch of sea salt makes for a delectable treat that's both indulgent and satisfying.

Pretzel M&M Cookies

Ingredients:

- **Dry Ingredients:**
    - 2 1/4 cups all-purpose flour
    - 1/2 teaspoon baking soda
    - 1/2 teaspoon baking powder
    - 1/4 teaspoon salt
- **Wet Ingredients:**
    - 1 cup (2 sticks) unsalted butter, room temperature
    - 1 cup granulated sugar
    - 1/2 cup packed brown sugar
    - 1 large egg
    - 1 teaspoon vanilla extract
- **Add-ins:**
    - 1 cup M&Ms (plain or peanut)
    - 1 cup pretzel pieces (broken into small chunks)

Instructions:

1. **Preheat Oven:**
    - Preheat your oven to 350°F (175°C). Line baking sheets with parchment paper or silicone baking mats.
2. **Mix Dry Ingredients:**
    - In a medium bowl, whisk together flour, baking soda, baking powder, and salt. Set aside.
3. **Cream Butter and Sugars:**
    - In a large bowl, use an electric mixer to cream together the butter, granulated sugar, and brown sugar until light and fluffy, about 2-3 minutes.
4. **Add Egg and Vanilla:**
    - Beat in the egg until fully incorporated. Mix in the vanilla extract until smooth.
5. **Combine Wet and Dry Ingredients:**
    - Gradually add the dry ingredients to the wet ingredients, mixing just until combined.
6. **Fold in M&Ms and Pretzels:**
    - Gently fold in the M&Ms and pretzel pieces until evenly distributed throughout the dough.
7. **Form Cookies:**
    - Using a cookie scoop or tablespoon, drop rounded balls of dough onto the prepared baking sheets, spacing them about 2 inches apart. Flatten each ball slightly with the back of a spoon.
8. **Bake:**

- Bake in the preheated oven for 10-12 minutes, or until the edges are lightly golden and the centers are set. The cookies will continue to firm up as they cool.
9. **Cool:**
    - Allow the cookies to cool on the baking sheets for about 5 minutes before transferring them to a wire rack to cool completely.

Tips:

- **Pretzels:** Use pretzel twists or pretzel sticks, broken into small chunks. Avoid using pretzel crumbs, as they may not provide the desired crunch.
- **M&Ms:** You can use plain or peanut M&Ms, depending on your preference. If using peanut M&Ms, consider chopping them slightly for more even distribution.
- **Storage:** Store the cookies in an airtight container at room temperature for up to a week. They can also be frozen for longer storage.

Enjoy your homemade Pretzel M&M Cookies! The combination of sweet M&Ms, salty pretzels, and chewy cookie dough makes for a delightful treat that's sure to satisfy your cravings.

Brown Butter Chocolate Chip Cookies

Ingredients:

- **Dry Ingredients:**
    - 2 1/4 cups all-purpose flour
    - 1/2 teaspoon baking soda
    - 1/2 teaspoon baking powder
    - 1/4 teaspoon salt
- **Wet Ingredients:**
    - 1 cup (2 sticks) unsalted butter
    - 1 cup granulated sugar
    - 1/2 cup packed brown sugar
    - 1 large egg
    - 1 teaspoon vanilla extract
- **Add-ins:**
    - 1 1/2 cups semisweet chocolate chips or chunks

Instructions:

1. **Brown the Butter:**
    - In a medium saucepan over medium heat, melt the butter. Continue to cook, swirling the pan occasionally, until the butter foams and then turns a golden-brown color with a nutty aroma. This should take about 5-7 minutes. Remove from heat and let the browned butter cool slightly.
2. **Preheat Oven:**
    - Preheat your oven to 350°F (175°C). Line baking sheets with parchment paper or silicone baking mats.
3. **Mix Dry Ingredients:**
    - In a medium bowl, whisk together flour, baking soda, baking powder, and salt. Set aside.
4. **Combine Sugars and Brown Butter:**
    - In a large bowl, mix the granulated sugar, brown sugar, and browned butter until well combined and smooth.
5. **Add Egg and Vanilla:**
    - Beat in the egg until fully incorporated. Mix in the vanilla extract.
6. **Combine Wet and Dry Ingredients:**
    - Gradually add the dry ingredients to the wet ingredients, mixing just until combined.
7. **Fold in Chocolate Chips:**
    - Gently fold in the chocolate chips or chunks until evenly distributed throughout the dough.
8. **Form Cookies:**

- Using a cookie scoop or tablespoon, drop rounded balls of dough onto the prepared baking sheets, spacing them about 2 inches apart. Flatten each ball slightly with the back of a spoon if desired.

9. **Bake:**
    - Bake in the preheated oven for 10-12 minutes, or until the edges are lightly golden and the centers are set. The cookies will continue to firm up as they cool.

10. **Cool:**
    - Allow the cookies to cool on the baking sheets for about 5 minutes before transferring them to a wire rack to cool completely.

Tips:

- **Cooling Butter:** Make sure the browned butter is slightly cooled but still liquid when mixing with the sugars. If it's too hot, it can cause the sugars to dissolve too quickly.
- **Texture:** For a chewier texture, avoid overbaking. The cookies should look slightly underbaked in the center when you remove them from the oven.
- **Storage:** Store the cookies in an airtight container at room temperature for up to a week, or freeze for longer storage.

Enjoy your Brown Butter Chocolate Chip Cookies! The rich, nutty flavor of the browned butter adds a delicious twist to the classic chocolate chip cookie, making these treats extra special.

Matcha Green Tea Cookies

Ingredients:

- **Dry Ingredients:**
    - 2 cups all-purpose flour
    - 2 tablespoons matcha green tea powder
    - 1/2 teaspoon baking soda
    - 1/2 teaspoon baking powder
    - 1/4 teaspoon salt
- **Wet Ingredients:**
    - 1 cup (2 sticks) unsalted butter, room temperature
    - 1 cup granulated sugar
    - 1/2 cup packed brown sugar
    - 1 large egg
    - 1 teaspoon vanilla extract
- **Optional Add-ins:**
    - 1/2 cup white chocolate chips or chopped white chocolate

Instructions:

1. **Preheat Oven:**
    - Preheat your oven to 350°F (175°C). Line baking sheets with parchment paper or silicone baking mats.
2. **Mix Dry Ingredients:**
    - In a medium bowl, whisk together flour, matcha powder, baking soda, baking powder, and salt. Set aside.
3. **Cream Butter and Sugars:**
    - In a large bowl, use an electric mixer to cream together the butter, granulated sugar, and brown sugar until light and fluffy, about 2-3 minutes.
4. **Add Egg and Vanilla:**
    - Beat in the egg until fully incorporated. Mix in the vanilla extract until smooth.
5. **Combine Wet and Dry Ingredients:**
    - Gradually add the dry ingredients to the wet ingredients, mixing just until combined.
6. **Fold in Optional Add-ins:**
    - If using, gently fold in the white chocolate chips or chopped white chocolate until evenly distributed throughout the dough.
7. **Form Cookies:**
    - Using a cookie scoop or tablespoon, drop rounded balls of dough onto the prepared baking sheets, spacing them about 2 inches apart. Flatten each ball slightly with the back of a spoon if desired.
8. **Bake:**

- Bake in the preheated oven for 10-12 minutes, or until the edges are lightly golden and the centers are set. The cookies will continue to firm up as they cool.
9. **Cool:**
    - Allow the cookies to cool on the baking sheets for about 5 minutes before transferring them to a wire rack to cool completely.

Tips:

- Matcha Quality: Use high-quality culinary-grade matcha powder for the best flavor and color.
- Mixing: Ensure the matcha powder is well mixed with the dry ingredients to avoid clumping.
- Texture: The cookies will have a slightly different texture due to the matcha powder. They should be soft and chewy with a subtle green tea flavor.
- Storage: Store the cookies in an airtight container at room temperature for up to a week, or freeze for longer storage.

Enjoy your homemade Matcha Green Tea Cookies! They offer a unique and elegant twist on traditional cookies, with a lovely green hue and the distinct taste of matcha.

Puffed Rice Cookies

Ingredients:

- **Dry Ingredients:**
    - 1 3/4 cups all-purpose flour
    - 1/2 teaspoon baking soda
    - 1/4 teaspoon salt
- **Wet Ingredients:**
    - 1 cup (2 sticks) unsalted butter, room temperature
    - 1 cup granulated sugar
    - 1/2 cup packed brown sugar
    - 1 large egg
    - 1 teaspoon vanilla extract
- **Add-ins:**
    - 2 cups puffed rice cereal (like Rice Krispies)
    - 1/2 cup chocolate chips or chunks (optional)

Instructions:

1. **Preheat Oven:**
    - Preheat your oven to 350°F (175°C). Line baking sheets with parchment paper or silicone baking mats.
2. **Mix Dry Ingredients:**
    - In a medium bowl, whisk together flour, baking soda, and salt. Set aside.
3. **Cream Butter and Sugars:**
    - In a large bowl, use an electric mixer to cream together the butter, granulated sugar, and brown sugar until light and fluffy, about 2-3 minutes.
4. **Add Egg and Vanilla:**
    - Beat in the egg until fully incorporated. Mix in the vanilla extract until smooth.
5. **Combine Wet and Dry Ingredients:**
    - Gradually add the dry ingredients to the wet ingredients, mixing just until combined.
6. **Fold in Puffed Rice and Optional Chocolate Chips:**
    - Gently fold in the puffed rice cereal and chocolate chips or chunks if using, until evenly distributed throughout the dough.
7. **Form Cookies:**
    - Using a cookie scoop or tablespoon, drop rounded balls of dough onto the prepared baking sheets, spacing them about 2 inches apart. Flatten each ball slightly with the back of a spoon.
8. **Bake:**
    - Bake in the preheated oven for 10-12 minutes, or until the edges are lightly golden and the centers are set. The cookies will continue to firm up as they cool.
9. **Cool:**

- Allow the cookies to cool on the baking sheets for about 5 minutes before transferring them to a wire rack to cool completely.

Tips:

- **Puffed Rice:** Use plain puffed rice cereal for a neutral flavor that pairs well with the cookie dough. Avoid using sweetened cereals.
- **Mixing:** Be gentle when folding in the puffed rice to avoid crushing them and losing their crunch.
- **Texture:** The cookies will have a unique texture with a nice crunch from the puffed rice. They should be soft and chewy with a crisp edge.
- **Storage:** Store the cookies in an airtight container at room temperature for up to a week. They can also be frozen for longer storage.

Enjoy your Puffed Rice Cookies! They offer a fun crunch and a delightful twist on traditional cookie recipes.

Cherry Almond Cookies

Ingredients:

- **Dry Ingredients:**
    - 2 1/4 cups all-purpose flour
    - 1/2 teaspoon baking soda
    - 1/4 teaspoon salt
- **Wet Ingredients:**
    - 1 cup (2 sticks) unsalted butter, room temperature
    - 1 cup granulated sugar
    - 1/2 cup packed brown sugar
    - 1 large egg
    - 1 teaspoon vanilla extract
    - 1 teaspoon almond extract
- **Add-ins:**
    - 1 cup dried cherries, chopped if large
    - 1/2 cup sliced almonds

Instructions:

1. **Preheat Oven:**
    - Preheat your oven to 350°F (175°C). Line baking sheets with parchment paper or silicone baking mats.
2. **Mix Dry Ingredients:**
    - In a medium bowl, whisk together flour, baking soda, and salt. Set aside.
3. **Cream Butter and Sugars:**
    - In a large bowl, use an electric mixer to cream together the butter, granulated sugar, and brown sugar until light and fluffy, about 2-3 minutes.
4. **Add Egg and Extracts:**
    - Beat in the egg until fully incorporated. Mix in the vanilla extract and almond extract until smooth.
5. **Combine Wet and Dry Ingredients:**
    - Gradually add the dry ingredients to the wet ingredients, mixing just until combined.
6. **Fold in Cherries and Almonds:**
    - Gently fold in the dried cherries and sliced almonds until evenly distributed throughout the dough.
7. **Form Cookies:**
    - Using a cookie scoop or tablespoon, drop rounded balls of dough onto the prepared baking sheets, spacing them about 2 inches apart. Flatten each ball slightly with the back of a spoon.
8. **Bake:**

- Bake in the preheated oven for 10-12 minutes, or until the edges are lightly golden and the centers are set. The cookies will continue to firm up as they cool.
9. **Cool:**
    - Allow the cookies to cool on the baking sheets for about 5 minutes before transferring them to a wire rack to cool completely.

Tips:

- **Cherries:** If the dried cherries are very large, consider chopping them into smaller pieces to ensure even distribution throughout the dough.
- **Almonds:** Lightly toasting the sliced almonds before adding them to the dough can enhance their flavor and crunch.
- **Texture:** The cookies should be soft and chewy with a slightly crisp edge. Don't overbake to maintain the desired texture.
- **Storage:** Store the cookies in an airtight container at room temperature for up to a week. They can also be frozen for longer storage.

Enjoy your Cherry Almond Cookies! The combination of sweet cherries and nutty almonds makes for a delicious and satisfying treat.

Apricot Almond Cookies

Ingredients:

- **Dry Ingredients:**
    - 1 3/4 cups all-purpose flour
    - 1/2 teaspoon baking soda
    - 1/4 teaspoon salt
- **Wet Ingredients:**
    - 1 cup (2 sticks) unsalted butter, room temperature
    - 1 cup granulated sugar
    - 1/2 cup packed brown sugar
    - 1 large egg
    - 1 teaspoon vanilla extract
    - 1 teaspoon almond extract
- **Add-ins:**
    - 1 cup dried apricots, chopped into small pieces
    - 1/2 cup sliced almonds

Instructions:

1. **Preheat Oven:**
    - Preheat your oven to 350°F (175°C). Line baking sheets with parchment paper or silicone baking mats.
2. **Mix Dry Ingredients:**
    - In a medium bowl, whisk together flour, baking soda, and salt. Set aside.
3. **Cream Butter and Sugars:**
    - In a large bowl, use an electric mixer to cream together the butter, granulated sugar, and brown sugar until light and fluffy, about 2-3 minutes.
4. **Add Egg and Extracts:**
    - Beat in the egg until fully incorporated. Mix in the vanilla extract and almond extract until smooth.
5. **Combine Wet and Dry Ingredients:**
    - Gradually add the dry ingredients to the wet ingredients, mixing just until combined.
6. **Fold in Apricots and Almonds:**
    - Gently fold in the chopped dried apricots and sliced almonds until evenly distributed throughout the dough.
7. **Form Cookies:**
    - Using a cookie scoop or tablespoon, drop rounded balls of dough onto the prepared baking sheets, spacing them about 2 inches apart. Flatten each ball slightly with the back of a spoon.
8. **Bake:**

- Bake in the preheated oven for 10-12 minutes, or until the edges are lightly golden and the centers are set. The cookies will continue to firm up as they cool.
9. **Cool:**
    - Allow the cookies to cool on the baking sheets for about 5 minutes before transferring them to a wire rack to cool completely.

Tips:

- **Apricots:** If the dried apricots are very firm or dry, consider soaking them in warm water for about 10 minutes, then draining and chopping them before adding to the dough.
- **Almonds:** Lightly toasting the sliced almonds can enhance their flavor and add a bit of extra crunch to the cookies.
- **Texture:** These cookies should be soft and chewy with a slightly crisp edge. Avoid overbaking to maintain the desired texture.
- **Storage:** Store the cookies in an airtight container at room temperature for up to a week. They can also be frozen for longer storage.

Enjoy your Apricot Almond Cookies! The combination of sweet apricots and nutty almonds makes for a delicious and unique treat that's sure to delight.

Hazelnut Chocolate Cookies

Ingredients:

- **Dry Ingredients:**
    - 1 3/4 cups all-purpose flour
    - 1/2 teaspoon baking soda
    - 1/4 teaspoon salt
- **Wet Ingredients:**
    - 1 cup (2 sticks) unsalted butter, room temperature
    - 1 cup granulated sugar
    - 1/2 cup packed brown sugar
    - 1 large egg
    - 1 teaspoon vanilla extract
- **Add-ins:**
    - 1 cup semisweet chocolate chips or chunks
    - 1 cup chopped hazelnuts (toasted, if desired)

Instructions:

1. **Preheat Oven:**
    - Preheat your oven to 350°F (175°C). Line baking sheets with parchment paper or silicone baking mats.
2. **Mix Dry Ingredients:**
    - In a medium bowl, whisk together flour, baking soda, and salt. Set aside.
3. **Cream Butter and Sugars:**
    - In a large bowl, use an electric mixer to cream together the butter, granulated sugar, and brown sugar until light and fluffy, about 2-3 minutes.
4. **Add Egg and Vanilla:**
    - Beat in the egg until fully incorporated. Mix in the vanilla extract until smooth.
5. **Combine Wet and Dry Ingredients:**
    - Gradually add the dry ingredients to the wet ingredients, mixing just until combined.
6. **Fold in Chocolate and Hazelnuts:**
    - Gently fold in the chocolate chips or chunks and chopped hazelnuts until evenly distributed throughout the dough.
7. **Form Cookies:**
    - Using a cookie scoop or tablespoon, drop rounded balls of dough onto the prepared baking sheets, spacing them about 2 inches apart. Flatten each ball slightly with the back of a spoon.
8. **Bake:**
    - Bake in the preheated oven for 10-12 minutes, or until the edges are lightly golden and the centers are set. The cookies will continue to firm up as they cool.
9. **Cool:**

- Allow the cookies to cool on the baking sheets for about 5 minutes before transferring them to a wire rack to cool completely.

Tips:

- **Hazelnuts:** For extra flavor, toast the hazelnuts in a dry skillet over medium heat until fragrant and lightly browned. Let them cool before chopping and adding to the dough.
- **Chocolate:** You can use semisweet or dark chocolate chips or chunks based on your preference. Chopping a chocolate bar into chunks can add a rustic texture.
- **Texture:** The cookies should be soft and chewy with a nice crunch from the hazelnuts. Avoid overbaking to keep them tender.
- **Storage:** Store the cookies in an airtight container at room temperature for up to a week. They can also be frozen for longer storage.

Enjoy your Hazelnut Chocolate Cookies! The combination of rich chocolate and crunchy hazelnuts makes for a deliciously indulgent treat.

Espresso Chocolate Chip Cookies

Ingredients:

- **Dry Ingredients:**
    - 2 1/4 cups all-purpose flour
    - 1/2 teaspoon baking soda
    - 1/2 teaspoon baking powder
    - 1/4 teaspoon salt
- **Wet Ingredients:**
    - 1 cup (2 sticks) unsalted butter, room temperature
    - 1 cup granulated sugar
    - 1/2 cup packed brown sugar
    - 1 large egg
    - 1 tablespoon instant espresso powder
    - 1 teaspoon vanilla extract
- **Add-ins:**
    - 1 1/2 cups semisweet chocolate chips or chunks

Instructions:

1. **Preheat Oven:**
    - Preheat your oven to 350°F (175°C). Line baking sheets with parchment paper or silicone baking mats.
2. **Mix Dry Ingredients:**
    - In a medium bowl, whisk together flour, baking soda, baking powder, and salt. Set aside.
3. **Prepare Espresso:**
    - Dissolve the instant espresso powder in a small amount of hot water (about 1 tablespoon) to make a concentrated espresso. Let it cool slightly.
4. **Cream Butter and Sugars:**
    - In a large bowl, use an electric mixer to cream together the butter, granulated sugar, and brown sugar until light and fluffy, about 2-3 minutes.
5. **Add Egg, Espresso, and Vanilla:**
    - Beat in the egg until fully incorporated. Mix in the dissolved espresso and vanilla extract until smooth.
6. **Combine Wet and Dry Ingredients:**
    - Gradually add the dry ingredients to the wet ingredients, mixing just until combined.
7. **Fold in Chocolate Chips:**
    - Gently fold in the chocolate chips or chunks until evenly distributed throughout the dough.
8. **Form Cookies:**

- Using a cookie scoop or tablespoon, drop rounded balls of dough onto the prepared baking sheets, spacing them about 2 inches apart. Flatten each ball slightly with the back of a spoon if desired.

9. **Bake:**
   - Bake in the preheated oven for 10-12 minutes, or until the edges are lightly golden and the centers are set. The cookies will continue to firm up as they cool.
10. **Cool:**
    - Allow the cookies to cool on the baking sheets for about 5 minutes before transferring them to a wire rack to cool completely.

Tips:

- **Espresso Powder:** Instant espresso powder gives a strong coffee flavor. If you prefer a milder coffee taste, you can adjust the amount of espresso powder.
- **Mixing:** Ensure that the espresso is well incorporated into the dough to evenly distribute the coffee flavor.
- **Texture:** These cookies should be soft and chewy with a rich chocolate flavor and a subtle coffee kick. Avoid overbaking to maintain the tender texture.
- **Storage:** Store the cookies in an airtight container at room temperature for up to a week. They can also be frozen for longer storage.

Enjoy your Espresso Chocolate Chip Cookies! The espresso adds a delicious depth of flavor that pairs wonderfully with the chocolate, making these cookies a perfect treat for coffee lovers.

S'mores Sandwich Cookies

Ingredients:

For the Cookies:

- **Dry Ingredients:**
    - 1 1/2 cups all-purpose flour
    - 1 cup graham cracker crumbs (about 8 graham crackers, crushed)
    - 1/2 teaspoon baking soda
    - 1/4 teaspoon salt
- **Wet Ingredients:**
    - 1/2 cup (1 stick) unsalted butter, room temperature
    - 1/2 cup granulated sugar
    - 1/2 cup packed brown sugar
    - 1 large egg
    - 1 teaspoon vanilla extract

For the Filling:

- **Marshmallow Filling:**
    - 1 cup mini marshmallows (or 1 cup marshmallow fluff)
    - 1 tablespoon unsalted butter
- **Chocolate Layer:**
    - 1 cup semisweet chocolate chips
    - 2 tablespoons heavy cream

Instructions:

1. **Preheat Oven:**
    - Preheat your oven to 350°F (175°C). Line baking sheets with parchment paper or silicone baking mats.
2. **Mix Dry Ingredients:**
    - In a medium bowl, whisk together flour, graham cracker crumbs, baking soda, and salt. Set aside.
3. **Cream Butter and Sugars:**
    - In a large bowl, use an electric mixer to cream together the butter, granulated sugar, and brown sugar until light and fluffy, about 2-3 minutes.
4. **Add Egg and Vanilla:**
    - Beat in the egg until fully incorporated. Mix in the vanilla extract until smooth.
5. **Combine Wet and Dry Ingredients:**
    - Gradually add the dry ingredients to the wet ingredients, mixing just until combined.
6. **Form Cookies:**

- Using a cookie scoop or tablespoon, drop rounded balls of dough onto the prepared baking sheets, spacing them about 2 inches apart. Flatten each ball slightly with the back of a spoon.
7. **Bake:**
   - Bake in the preheated oven for 10-12 minutes, or until the edges are lightly golden. The centers should be set but soft. Allow the cookies to cool on the baking sheets for about 5 minutes before transferring them to a wire rack to cool completely.
8. **Prepare Marshmallow Filling:**
   - In a small saucepan over medium heat, melt the butter and add the mini marshmallows. Stir constantly until the marshmallows are melted and smooth. Remove from heat and let cool slightly.
9. **Prepare Chocolate Layer:**
   - In a microwave-safe bowl, combine the chocolate chips and heavy cream. Microwave in 30-second intervals, stirring in between, until the chocolate is fully melted and smooth.
10. **Assemble Sandwich Cookies:**
    - Spread a layer of the marshmallow filling on the bottom side of one cookie. Top with another cookie to make a sandwich. Repeat with the remaining cookies.
11. **Dip in Chocolate (Optional):**
    - If desired, dip the edges of each cookie sandwich into the melted chocolate and let the excess drip off. Place the cookies on a parchment-lined tray to set until the chocolate is firm.

Tips:

- **Marshmallow Filling:** If using marshmallow fluff, you can skip the melting step and just spread it directly onto the cookies.
- **Chocolate Layer:** Ensure the chocolate is smooth and well-mixed for a nice dip or drizzle.
- **Texture:** These cookies are best enjoyed fresh, as the marshmallow filling can become gooey over time.
- **Storage:** Store the assembled cookies in an airtight container at room temperature for up to 2-3 days. If you plan to store them for longer, it's best to keep the marshmallow filling and chocolate layer separate until ready to serve.

Enjoy your S'mores Sandwich Cookies! They offer a delightful twist on the classic s'mores treat with the added fun of being a cookie sandwich.

Almond Butter Cookies

Ingredients:

- **Dry Ingredients:**
    - 1 1/2 cups all-purpose flour
    - 1/2 teaspoon baking soda
    - 1/4 teaspoon salt
- **Wet Ingredients:**
    - 1/2 cup (1 stick) unsalted butter, room temperature
    - 1/2 cup almond butter (smooth or chunky)
    - 1/2 cup granulated sugar
    - 1/2 cup packed brown sugar
    - 1 large egg
    - 1 teaspoon vanilla extract

Instructions:

1. **Preheat Oven:**
    - Preheat your oven to 350°F (175°C). Line baking sheets with parchment paper or silicone baking mats.
2. **Mix Dry Ingredients:**
    - In a medium bowl, whisk together flour, baking soda, and salt. Set aside.
3. **Cream Butter, Almond Butter, and Sugars:**
    - In a large bowl, use an electric mixer to cream together the butter, almond butter, granulated sugar, and brown sugar until light and fluffy, about 2-3 minutes.
4. **Add Egg and Vanilla:**
    - Beat in the egg until fully incorporated. Mix in the vanilla extract until smooth.
5. **Combine Wet and Dry Ingredients:**
    - Gradually add the dry ingredients to the wet ingredients, mixing just until combined.
6. **Form Cookies:**
    - Using a cookie scoop or tablespoon, drop rounded balls of dough onto the prepared baking sheets, spacing them about 2 inches apart. Flatten each ball slightly with the back of a spoon or the tines of a fork.
7. **Bake:**
    - Bake in the preheated oven for 10-12 minutes, or until the edges are lightly golden and the centers are set. The cookies will continue to firm up as they cool.
8. **Cool:**
    - Allow the cookies to cool on the baking sheets for about 5 minutes before transferring them to a wire rack to cool completely.

Tips:

- **Almond Butter:** Use smooth almond butter for a uniform texture in the cookies. If using chunky almond butter, the cookies will have more texture and a bit more crunch.
- **Flavor Variations:** For extra flavor, you can add a pinch of cinnamon or a handful of chocolate chips or chopped almonds to the dough.
- **Texture:** The cookies should be soft and chewy with a rich almond flavor. Avoid overbaking to keep them tender.
- **Storage:** Store the cookies in an airtight container at room temperature for up to a week. They can also be frozen for longer storage.

Enjoy your Almond Butter Cookies! They offer a delightful twist on classic cookies with their nutty, rich flavor.

Zucchini Cookies

Ingredients:

- **Dry Ingredients:**
    - 1 1/2 cups all-purpose flour
    - 1 teaspoon baking powder
    - 1/2 teaspoon baking soda
    - 1/2 teaspoon ground cinnamon
    - 1/4 teaspoon salt
- **Wet Ingredients:**
    - 1/2 cup (1 stick) unsalted butter, room temperature
    - 1/2 cup granulated sugar
    - 1/2 cup packed brown sugar
    - 1 large egg
    - 1 teaspoon vanilla extract
    - 1 cup grated zucchini (about 1 small zucchini, squeezed dry)
- **Add-ins (Optional):**
    - 1/2 cup chocolate chips, raisins, or chopped nuts (such as walnuts or pecans)

Instructions:

1. **Preheat Oven:**
    - Preheat your oven to 350°F (175°C). Line baking sheets with parchment paper or silicone baking mats.
2. **Prepare Zucchini:**
    - Grate the zucchini using a box grater or food processor. Place the grated zucchini in a clean kitchen towel and squeeze out excess moisture. This step is important to prevent the cookies from becoming too soggy.
3. **Mix Dry Ingredients:**
    - In a medium bowl, whisk together flour, baking powder, baking soda, cinnamon, and salt. Set aside.
4. **Cream Butter and Sugars:**
    - In a large bowl, use an electric mixer to cream together the butter, granulated sugar, and brown sugar until light and fluffy, about 2-3 minutes.
5. **Add Egg and Vanilla:**
    - Beat in the egg until fully incorporated. Mix in the vanilla extract until smooth.
6. **Combine Wet and Dry Ingredients:**
    - Gradually add the dry ingredients to the wet ingredients, mixing just until combined.
7. **Fold in Zucchini and Optional Add-ins:**
    - Gently fold in the grated zucchini and any optional add-ins (chocolate chips, raisins, or nuts) until evenly distributed throughout the dough.
8. **Form Cookies:**

- Using a cookie scoop or tablespoon, drop rounded balls of dough onto the prepared baking sheets, spacing them about 2 inches apart. Flatten each ball slightly with the back of a spoon.

9. **Bake:**
   - Bake in the preheated oven for 10-12 minutes, or until the edges are lightly golden and the centers are set. The cookies will continue to firm up as they cool.

10. **Cool:**
    - Allow the cookies to cool on the baking sheets for about 5 minutes before transferring them to a wire rack to cool completely.

Tips:

- **Zucchini Preparation:** Ensure the zucchini is well-drained to avoid excess moisture in the dough. Squeeze it out thoroughly before adding it to the batter.
- **Add-ins:** Feel free to customize the cookies with your favorite mix-ins like chocolate chips, nuts, or dried fruit.
- **Texture:** These cookies are soft and moist. They may appear a little underbaked when you first take them out of the oven, but they will firm up as they cool.
- **Storage:** Store the cookies in an airtight container at room temperature for up to a week. They can also be frozen for longer storage.

Enjoy your Zucchini Cookies! They're a delicious, slightly healthier treat that makes great use of fresh zucchini.

Vegan Chocolate Chip Cookies

Ingredients:

- **Dry Ingredients:**
    - 1 1/2 cups all-purpose flour
    - 1/2 teaspoon baking soda
    - 1/4 teaspoon salt
- **Wet Ingredients:**
    - 1/2 cup coconut oil or vegan butter, solid (not melted)
    - 1/2 cup granulated sugar
    - 1/2 cup packed brown sugar
    - 1/4 cup non-dairy milk (such as almond, soy, or oat milk)
    - 1 tablespoon ground flaxseed mixed with 3 tablespoons water (flax egg)
    - 1 teaspoon vanilla extract
- **Add-ins:**
    - 1 cup vegan chocolate chips or chunks

Instructions:

1. **Preheat Oven:**
    - Preheat your oven to 350°F (175°C). Line baking sheets with parchment paper or silicone baking mats.
2. **Prepare Flax Egg:**
    - In a small bowl, mix the ground flaxseed with water and let it sit for about 5 minutes until it becomes gel-like.
3. **Mix Dry Ingredients:**
    - In a medium bowl, whisk together flour, baking soda, and salt. Set aside.
4. **Cream Vegan Butter and Sugars:**
    - In a large bowl, use an electric mixer to cream together the solid coconut oil or vegan butter, granulated sugar, and brown sugar until smooth and creamy, about 2-3 minutes.
5. **Add Flax Egg, Non-Dairy Milk, and Vanilla:**
    - Beat in the flax egg, non-dairy milk, and vanilla extract until fully incorporated.
6. **Combine Wet and Dry Ingredients:**
    - Gradually add the dry ingredients to the wet ingredients, mixing just until combined.
7. **Fold in Chocolate Chips:**
    - Gently fold in the vegan chocolate chips or chunks until evenly distributed throughout the dough.
8. **Form Cookies:**
    - Using a cookie scoop or tablespoon, drop rounded balls of dough onto the prepared baking sheets, spacing them about 2 inches apart. Flatten each ball slightly with the back of a spoon.

9. **Bake:**
    - Bake in the preheated oven for 10-12 minutes, or until the edges are lightly golden and the centers are set. The cookies will continue to firm up as they cool.
10. **Cool:**
    - Allow the cookies to cool on the baking sheets for about 5 minutes before transferring them to a wire rack to cool completely.

Tips:

- **Vegan Butter:** If you prefer using vegan butter, ensure it's solid but not melted for proper texture in the cookies.
- **Flax Egg:** The flax egg acts as a binder in place of traditional eggs. Make sure to let it sit for a few minutes to achieve the right consistency.
- **Texture:** These cookies are best enjoyed fresh, as they can become a bit softer over time due to the vegan ingredients. However, they should still be soft and chewy with a slight crisp edge.
- **Storage:** Store the cookies in an airtight container at room temperature for up to a week. They can also be frozen for longer storage.

Enjoy your Vegan Chocolate Chip Cookies! They're a delightful treat that proves you don't need eggs or dairy to make delicious cookies.

Gluten-Free Peanut Butter Cookies

Ingredients:

- **Wet Ingredients:**
    - 1 cup creamy or chunky peanut butter (make sure it's gluten-free)
    - 1/2 cup granulated sugar
    - 1/2 cup packed brown sugar
    - 1 large egg
    - 1 teaspoon vanilla extract
- **Optional Add-ins:**
    - 1/2 cup chocolate chips or chunks (ensure they are gluten-free)

Instructions:

1. **Preheat Oven:**
    - Preheat your oven to 350°F (175°C). Line baking sheets with parchment paper or silicone baking mats.
2. **Mix Wet Ingredients:**
    - In a large bowl, combine the peanut butter, granulated sugar, and brown sugar. Use an electric mixer or whisk to mix until smooth and creamy.
3. **Add Egg and Vanilla:**
    - Beat in the egg and vanilla extract until well combined.
4. **Form Cookies:**
    - Using a cookie scoop or tablespoon, drop rounded balls of dough onto the prepared baking sheets, spacing them about 2 inches apart. Flatten each ball slightly with the back of a fork, creating a crisscross pattern on top.
5. **Bake:**
    - Bake in the preheated oven for 8-10 minutes, or until the edges are lightly golden. The centers should be set but still soft. The cookies will firm up as they cool.
6. **Cool:**
    - Allow the cookies to cool on the baking sheets for about 5 minutes before transferring them to a wire rack to cool completely.

Tips:

- **Peanut Butter:** Ensure that the peanut butter you use is labeled gluten-free, as some brands may contain trace gluten or cross-contamination.
- **Texture:** These cookies are typically very soft and chewy. Avoid overbaking to keep them from becoming too dry.
- **Add-ins:** If using chocolate chips, make sure they are labeled gluten-free. You can also add a pinch of sea salt on top of the cookies before baking for extra flavor.

- **Storage:** Store the cookies in an airtight container at room temperature for up to a week. They can also be frozen for longer storage.

Enjoy your Gluten-Free Peanut Butter Cookies! They are a classic treat that's naturally free of gluten and sure to satisfy your sweet tooth.

Strawberry Shortcake Cookies

Ingredients:

- **Dry Ingredients:**
    - 2 cups all-purpose flour
    - 1/2 teaspoon baking powder
    - 1/2 teaspoon baking soda
    - 1/4 teaspoon salt
- **Wet Ingredients:**
    - 1/2 cup (1 stick) unsalted butter, room temperature
    - 1/2 cup granulated sugar
    - 1/4 cup packed brown sugar
    - 1 large egg
    - 1 teaspoon vanilla extract
- **Add-ins:**
    - 1 cup fresh strawberries, chopped into small pieces
    - 1/2 cup white chocolate chips or chopped white chocolate (optional)
- **For the Topping:**
    - 2 tablespoons granulated sugar
    - 1/2 teaspoon ground cinnamon

Instructions:

1. **Preheat Oven:**
    - Preheat your oven to 350°F (175°C). Line baking sheets with parchment paper or silicone baking mats.
2. **Prepare Strawberries:**
    - Chop the strawberries into small pieces and pat them dry with a paper towel to remove excess moisture. This helps prevent the cookies from becoming soggy.
3. **Mix Dry Ingredients:**
    - In a medium bowl, whisk together flour, baking powder, baking soda, and salt. Set aside.
4. **Cream Butter and Sugars:**
    - In a large bowl, use an electric mixer to cream together the butter, granulated sugar, and brown sugar until light and fluffy, about 2-3 minutes.
5. **Add Egg and Vanilla:**
    - Beat in the egg until fully incorporated. Mix in the vanilla extract until smooth.
6. **Combine Wet and Dry Ingredients:**
    - Gradually add the dry ingredients to the wet ingredients, mixing just until combined.
7. **Fold in Strawberries and Optional Chocolate:**
    - Gently fold in the chopped strawberries and white chocolate chips, if using, until evenly distributed throughout the dough.

8. **Form Cookies:**
   - Using a cookie scoop or tablespoon, drop rounded balls of dough onto the prepared baking sheets, spacing them about 2 inches apart. Flatten each ball slightly with the back of a spoon.
9. **Prepare Topping:**
   - In a small bowl, mix together the granulated sugar and ground cinnamon. Sprinkle a small amount of this mixture over the top of each cookie.
10. **Bake:**
    - Bake in the preheated oven for 10-12 minutes, or until the edges are lightly golden and the centers are set. The cookies will firm up as they cool.
11. **Cool:**
    - Allow the cookies to cool on the baking sheets for about 5 minutes before transferring them to a wire rack to cool completely.

Tips:

- **Strawberries:** Make sure the strawberries are chopped into small pieces and dried to prevent excess moisture in the cookies.
- **White Chocolate:** If using, ensure the white chocolate is chopped into small pieces for even distribution.
- **Texture:** These cookies should be soft and tender with a delightful burst of strawberry flavor. Avoid overbaking to keep them soft.
- **Storage:** Store the cookies in an airtight container at room temperature for up to a week. They are best enjoyed fresh but can be frozen for longer storage.

Enjoy your Strawberry Shortcake Cookies! They offer a delicious twist on the classic dessert and are perfect for any occasion.

Chocolate Lava Cookies

Ingredients:

- **Dry Ingredients:**
    - 1 1/2 cups all-purpose flour
    - 1/2 teaspoon baking powder
    - 1/4 teaspoon salt
- **Wet Ingredients:**
    - 1/2 cup (1 stick) unsalted butter, room temperature
    - 1/2 cup granulated sugar
    - 1/2 cup packed brown sugar
    - 1 large egg
    - 1 teaspoon vanilla extract
- **Chocolate Lava Filling:**
    - 4 ounces semi-sweet chocolate, chopped
    - 1/4 cup heavy cream
    - 1 tablespoon unsalted butter
- **For the Topping (Optional):**
    - Powdered sugar for dusting

Instructions:

1. **Prepare Chocolate Lava Filling:**
    - In a small saucepan over low heat, combine the chopped chocolate, heavy cream, and butter. Stir until the chocolate is completely melted and smooth. Remove from heat and let it cool slightly, then chill in the refrigerator for about 30 minutes until firm.
2. **Preheat Oven:**
    - Preheat your oven to 350°F (175°C). Line baking sheets with parchment paper or silicone baking mats.
3. **Mix Dry Ingredients:**
    - In a medium bowl, whisk together flour, baking powder, and salt. Set aside.
4. **Cream Butter and Sugars:**
    - In a large bowl, use an electric mixer to cream together the butter, granulated sugar, and brown sugar until light and fluffy, about 2-3 minutes.
5. **Add Egg and Vanilla:**
    - Beat in the egg until fully incorporated. Mix in the vanilla extract until smooth.
6. **Combine Wet and Dry Ingredients:**
    - Gradually add the dry ingredients to the wet ingredients, mixing just until combined.
7. **Form Cookies:**
    - Take a small amount of cookie dough and flatten it in your hand. Place a teaspoon of the chilled chocolate lava filling in the center, then carefully wrap the

dough around the filling, sealing it completely. Roll into a ball and place on the prepared baking sheets. Repeat with the remaining dough and filling.

8. **Bake:**
   - Bake in the preheated oven for 10-12 minutes, or until the edges are lightly golden. The centers may look slightly underbaked, which is fine as they will firm up as they cool and the lava will remain gooey inside.
9. **Cool:**
   - Allow the cookies to cool on the baking sheets for about 5 minutes before transferring them to a wire rack to cool completely.
10. **Add Topping (Optional):**
    - Once cooled, dust the cookies with powdered sugar if desired for an extra touch of sweetness.

Tips:

- **Chocolate Filling:** Make sure the chocolate filling is chilled until firm to prevent it from leaking out too much during baking.
- **Handling Dough:** If the dough becomes too soft while working with it, you can chill it for a few minutes to make it easier to handle.
- **Texture:** These cookies should have a crisp exterior with a gooey chocolate center. Avoid overbaking to ensure the lava remains melted.

Enjoy your Chocolate Lava Cookies! They're a perfect indulgence for any chocolate lover and a great way to impress guests with a delicious surprise inside.

www.ingramcontent.com/pod-product-compliance
Lightning Source LLC
LaVergne TN
LVHW081600060526
838201LV00054B/1981